Collins Illustrated Guide to

XI'AN

Simon Holledge

Photography by Jacky Yip

COLLINS

8 Grafton Street, London W1
1988

William Collins Sons & Co. Ltd
London • Glasgow • Sydney • Auckland
Toronto • Johannesburg

British Library Cataloguing in Publication Data

Collins Illustrated Guide to Xi'an — (China Guides Series)
1. Xi'an (China) — Description and Travel —
Guide-books
I. Series
915.1'430458   DS796.X/

ISBN 0-00-215263-0

First published 1988
Copyright © The Guidebook Company Ltd. 1988

Series Editors: May Holdsworth and Jill Hunt
Picture Editor: Ingrid Morejohn

Revised by Seth Faison Jr and Julia Wilkinson
Additional text contributions by Min Dinning, May Holdsworth and Jill Hunt

Photography by Jacky Yip — China Photo Library, with additional contributions by:
Luo Zhong Min (10, 37, 53, 57, 60, 65, 68−9, 72, 73, 97); Yu Shi Jun (18−19);
China Photo Library (8−9, 40); Gary Chapman (48−9); Simon Holledge (83);
Ingrid Morejohn (101, 123); China Guides Series (23, 33, 44, 118)

The Guidebook Company wishes to express special thanks to the officials of the Shaanxi
Provincial Museum, Qin Terracotta Army Museum, Great Mosque, Shaanxi Foreign
Affairs Office, Shaanxi Tourism Bureau and the Qian Ling Museum

Design by Joan Law Design & Photography

Printed in Hong Kong

Contents

Special Topics

Maps

Names and Addresses

In this book addresses are given in *Pinyin. Dajie* is a main thoroughfare; *lu* is a road and *jie* is a street; *xiang* is a lane or alley.

To help visitors getting about on their own, names of hotels and restaurants are given in Chinese characters in the text, while names of all the sights, shops and other places described in the book are given in Chinese characters either in the Useful Addresses section or in the Index of Places.

An Introduction to Xi'an

David Bonavia

The city of Xi'an has at different times been the capital of China for longer than any other — a total of some 1,100 years. The magnificent archaeological and art discoveries in and around the city tell the tale of China's development from prehistoric times till the height of the imperial period. There have been so many astounding finds in the area that only a small proportion of them are as yet on view to the public, although a growing number are now being put on display.

Xi'an was at different times the capital of the Zhou, Han, Sui and Tang Dynasties. Lying on the Wei River in Shaanxi Province, it commanded the approaches to central China from the mountains of the northwest. It was also the starting point of the old Silk Road along which Chinese merchandise was taken as far west as the Mediterranean.

The modern city is plain and business-like, but the narrow residential alleys and street markets bear the flavour of old China. Sections of the old city wall testify to Xi'an's strategic importance down the ages.

Easily accessible from Xi'an is Yan'an, where the late Chairman Mao Zedong's followers in the Communist Party built up their strength for the final confrontation with Generalissimo Chiang Kai-shek's Nationalist forces. Chiang was actually captured in his nightgown trying to escape from a hot springs resort near Xi'an, by a younger commander who wanted him to unite with the Communists and fight the Japanese — the famous Xi'an Incident of 1936.

Dubbed 'the land of kings and emperors' by Du Fu, China's most famous poet, Xi'an can trace its origins to the 11th century BC, when the rulers of the Zhou Dynasty set up Fenghao, a twin city made up of Fengjing and Haojing, about 16 kilometres (ten miles) southwest of the present site. The city was grid-shaped — a pattern which later became common in Chinese cities. It was said that nine carts could ride abreast on each of the 18 main roads of the grid.

In the eighth century BC, the Zhou Dynasty moved its capital downstream to Luoyang. A ruler of the Kingdom of Qin, in northwest China, established his capital at Xianyang, just to the north of Xi'an. In 221 BC the King of Qin conquered the other feudal kingdoms to become the First Emperor. Qin Shihuangdi, as he became known, imposed an early form of totalitarianism on China. He consolidated and extended the various sections of the Great Wall which was meant to keep out fierce northern tribesmen. He standardized the Chinese written language and even the span of cart axles. But his oppressive rule broke down when his son succeeded to the throne, and after a bloody civil war a rebel commander called Liu Bang established the Han Dynasty with its capital at the city, which was now called Chang'an.

The Han Dynasty was a period of great cultural flowering and imperial expansion. Pottery, bronze and iron work, lacquer, precious metals, wall-painting and sculpture of a very high artistic standard survive in impressive quantities. Chang'an was three times the size of Rome at the time. Chinese and Roman soldiers may actually have crossed swords in central Asia, but this has not been proven.

Qin Shihuangdi died in 210 BC. In accordance with the custom of the time, it is believed, he had his ministers, family members, slaves and horses buried with him — but whether all of them were actually killed, as would have been normal a few centuries earlier, or whether some were buried later as they naturally died, is not clear. The main part of the tomb remains to be excavated.

But the pottery figures of soldiers and horses leave no doubt that the emperor wanted a bodyguard in the after-life. There are estimated to be fully 8,000 clay warriors, whose existence was discovered by some peasants digging a well in 1974. Each human figure is different from the other — or so it seems — and they are slightly larger than life-size. They wear a variety of uniforms and body-armour, though all have a flowing, knee-length robe, a turned-round lapel, and breeches. They wear their hair in elaborate topknots and sport moustaches. Some are kneeling in postures which suggest that they once held drawn bows of wood, now decayed. The whole tomb area covers nearly 57 square kilometres (22 square miles). There is an outer wall with four gates, and an inner wall with five — two of them being on the north side. The figures are a fascinating direct link with the past over a period of 22 centuries.

In AD 25 the Eastern Han Dynasty removed the capital to Luoyang. From the third century there ensued a period of civil war and division of China into separate kingdoms, sometimes with rival claimants to the title of Emperor. But in 582 the founder of the Sui Dynasty, Yang Qian, restored the city as the capital. It was enlarged and improved, and a famous Chinese poet wrote of it: 'Ten thousand houses look like a laid-out chessboard'. Merchants and tribute bearers from central and western Asia arrived there with exotic products. But the new capital shortly fell to Li Yuan, who established the Tang Dynasty. The most famous imperial concubine in Chinese history, the beauty Yang Guifei, and the most powerful empress, Wu Zetian, inhabited the imperial palace in the Tang Dynasty. In its cultural achievements, the Tang outdid even the Han Dynasty, especially in poetry, painting, music, ceramics and calligraphy.

With the fall of the Tang Dynasty in 907, the capital was removed — after a period of civil war — to the city of Kaifeng in Henan Province in AD 960, and later, when the Jin Tartars invaded north China, to Hangzhou in the east. In 1295 the Mongols led by Kublai Khan conquered all China and established their capital at Beijing. The Ming Dynasty (1368–1644), while governing from Beijing, rebuilt the inner section of the city now called Xi'an, but it was never to be the capital again.

The main tourist attractions of today's X'ian are the Ming-Dynasty Drum Tower and Bell Tower near the city centre, the Shaanxi Museum, the Big Goose and Little Goose Pagodas, the Great Mosque, the old city wall, the stone-age site at Banpo, and above all the pottery figures buried in the ground to 'guard' Qin Shihuangdi's tomb.

Numerous other imperial tombs are known to exist, though they may have been despoiled by tomb-robbers and will take time to excavate.

Though the city is quite heavily industrialized, the Chinese Government has decided to give priority to excavation and restoration of ancient sites and buildings. Unfortunately much damage has already been done to the old city, which cannot be restored. Nevertheless, the once-magnificent city walls have now been carefully repaired, and provide a spacious and open promenade around Xi'an for both citizens and visitors to enjoy.

Modern Xi'an

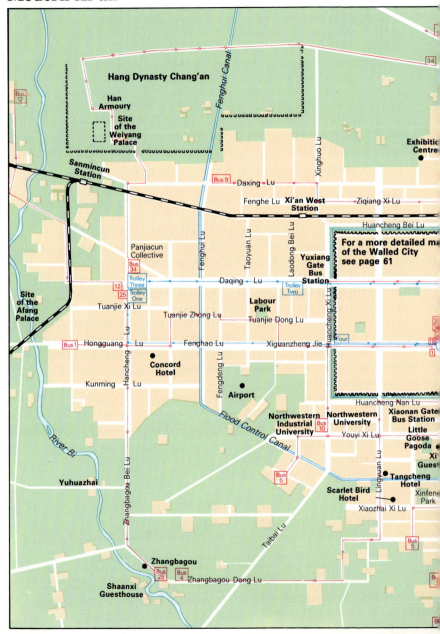

Hang Dynasty Chang'an

Han Armoury

Site of the Weiyang Palace

Sanmincun Station

Bus 12

Exhibition Centre

34

Bus 9 Daxing Lu

Fenghe Lu Xi'an West Station Ziqiang Xi Lu

Xinghuo Lu

Huancheng Bei Lu

Fenghui Canal

Panjiacun Collective

Bus 34

For a more detailed ma of the Walled City see page 61

Fenghui Lu

Taoyuan Lu

Laodong Bei Lu

Yuxiang Gate Bus Station

Trolley Three
Trolley One

12
25

Daqing Lu

Trolley Two

Site of the Afang Palace

Tuanjie Xi Lu

Tuanjie Zhong Lu

Labour Park

Tuanjie Dong Lu

Huancheng Xi Lu

3
3
18
1

Four

Bus 1 Hongguang Lu

Fenghao Lu

Xiguanzheng Jie

Hancheng Lu

Concord Hotel

Fengdeng Lu

Kunming Lu

Airport

Huancheng Nan Lu

Northwestern Industrial University

Northwestern University

Xiaonan Gate Bus Station

Little Goose Pagoda

Bus 10

Youyi Xi Lu

River Bi

Zhangbagou Bei Lu

Flood Control Canal

Bus 6

Lingyuan Lu

Xi Guest

Tangcheng Hotel

Yuhuazhai

Scarlet Bird Hotel

Xinfen Park

Xiaozhai Xi Lu

Taibai Lu

Bus 5

Bu

Zhangbagou

Bus 25
Bus 4

Zhangbagou Dong Lu

Shaanxi Guesthouse

Bu

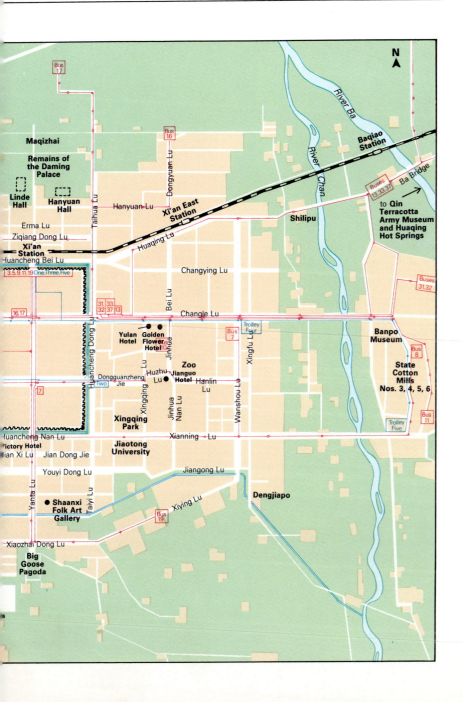

N

Bus 17

Maqizhai

Remains of
the Daming
Palace

Bus 16

Linde
Hall

Hanyuan
Hall

Dongyuan Lu

Baqiao
Station

River Ba

Ba Bridge

Erma Lu

Ziqiang Dong Lu

Taihua Lu

Hanyuan Lu

Xi'an East
Station

Huaqing Lu

River Chan

Buses
13·33·37

to Qin
Terracotta
Army Museum
and Huaqing
Hot Springs

Shilipu

Xi'an
Station

Huancheng Bei Lu

Changying Lu

Changle Lu

Buses
31·32

3·5·9·11·19 One Three Five

Bei Lu

16·17

31 33
32 37 13

Bus 8

Banpo
Museum

Yulan
Hotel

Golden
Flower
Hotel

Jinhua

Bus 7

Trolley
Four

Xingfu Lu

Huancheng Dong Lu

Dongguanzheng
Jie

Two

Zoo

Jianguo
Hotel

Hanlin
Lu

State
Cotton
Mills
Nos. 3, 4, 5, 6

Huzhu
Lu

Bus 11

7

Xingqing
Lu

Jinhua
Nan Lu

Wanshou Lu

Trolley
Five

Xingqing
Park

Xianning Lu

Huancheng Nan Lu

Victory Hotel

Jian Xi Lu

Jian Dong Jie

Jiaotong
University

Youyi Dong Lu

Jiangong Lu

Dengjiapo

Shaanxi
Folk Art
Gallery

Yanta Lu

Taiyi Lu

Xiying Lu

Bus 19

Xiaozhai Dong Lu

Big
Goose
Pagoda

Getting to Xi'an

Before the Second World War the few foreigners who made the
arduous journey to Xi'an considered themselves adventurers rather
than tourists. To reach their destination they had to travel to the end
of the railway line in the neighbouring province of Henan, and then
transfer to bumpy carts for a further journey of six days through
'bandit infested' country. The journey became easier when the railway
reached Xi'an in 1934. A new station was built only in 1986. Today
Xi'an has become the main communications centre for the northwest
region of China.

By Air The Chinese airline, CAAC (Civil Aviation Administration of
China) has a direct service from Hong Kong; frequency varies with the
season, with one flight a week in winter, and two or more, in summer.
Daily flights are available from Beijing (2 hours), Shanghai (2.75
hours) and Guangzhou (3 hours). There are also air connections with
Changsha, Chengdu, Chongqing, Kunming, Lanzhou, Nanjing,
Taiyuan and Zhengzhou.

   As eleswhere in China, planes are sometimes delayed for hours in
bad weather. But a new airport (able to take wide-bodied planes) in
the neighbouring town of Xianyang is scheduled to open in 1989 which
should help increase air capacity to Xi'an, and improve ground service
considerably.

By Rail Xi'an is on the main east—west railway that goes all the way
from Shanghai to the Xinjiang Uygur Autonomous Region, in the far
northwest of China. Express trains arrive daily from Beijing (taking
about 18 hours) and also from Shanghai, Nanjing, Qingdao,
Zhengzhou, Wuchang, Chongqing, Chengdu, Lanzhou, Urumqi,
Taiyuan and Guangzhou (travellers from Hong Kong can book
sleepers through CITS for the 34-hour trip from Guangzhou).
Luoyang, the historic 'Eastern Capital', is 387 kilometres (240 miles)
to the east of Xi'an. The journey takes seven hours and there are
trains every day.

General Information for Travellers

Visas

Everyone must get a visa to go to China, but this is usually an easy,
trouble-free process. Tourists travelling in a group are listed on a
single group visa — a special document listing all members of the

group — which is issued in advance to tour organizers. Individual passports of people travelling on a group visa will not be stamped unless specifically requested.

Tourist visas for individual travellers (those who are not travelling in a group) can be obtained directly through Chinese embassies and consulates, alhough some embassies are more enthusiastic about issuing them than others. Certain travel agents and tour operators around the world can arrange individual visas for their clients. It is simplest in Hong Kong, where there are a large number of travel agents handling visa applications. Just one passport photograph and a completed application form are necessary.

Visa fees vary considerably, depending on the source of the visa, and on the time taken to get it. In Hong Kong, for instance, some travel agents can get you a tourist visa in a few hours, but it may cost around US$30 for one valid for three months, while a one-month visa which takes 48 hours to obtain might cost just US$6.50.

The visa gives you automatic entry to all China's open cities and areas (there were 436 in 1987). Travel permits to certain areas of China, which used to be needed in addition to the visa, were dropped in 1986.

The mechanics of getting a business visa are much more flexible than in the past, particularly in Hong Kong. The applicant should have either an invitation from the appropriate Foreign Trade Corporation (several now have permanent representatives abroad), or from the organizers of a specialized trade fair or seminar. In Hong Kong, all that is needed is a letter from the applicant's company confirming that he wishes to travel to China on business.

Regular business visitors are eligible for a multiple re-entry visa which may be obtained with the help of a business contact in China. Some Hong Kong travel agents can also arrange re-entry visas for clients — the cost might be around US$50–60. This type of visa may be for three or six months.

Customs

A customs declaration form must be filled out by each visitor upon entry — the carbon copy of this form will be returned to you and it must be produced at customs for inspection on departure from China.

Some personal possessions that you are asked to list on arrival — such as tape recorders, cameras, watches and jewellery — must be taken out with you when you leave. When you arrive you will be told at immigration which items these are, and they may be inspected by customs officials on departure from China.

Four bottles of alcohol, three cartons of cigarettes, unlimited film and unlimited medicines for personal use may be taken in. Firearms and dangerous drugs are strictly forbidden.

Money

Chinese Currency The Chinese currency, which is sometimes referred to as Renminbi or Rmb, meaning 'people's currency', is denominated in *yuan* which are each divided into 10 *jiao*, colloquially called *mao*. Each *jiao* is, in turn, divided into 10 *fen*. There are large notes for 100, 50,10, 5, 2, and 1 *yuan*, small notes for 5, 2, and 1 *jiao*, and coins for 5, 2 and 1 *fen*.

Currency Certificates Foreign Exchange Certificates (FEC) were introduced in 1980. These were designed to be used instead of Renminbi by foreigners, Overseas Chinese and Chinese from Hong Kong and Macao only, for payments in hotels, Friendship Stores, at trade fairs, and for airline tickets, international phone calls, parcel post etc. In actual practice, however, FEC became a sought-after form of payment anywhere, and a black market developed between the two currencies. In September 1986 the Chinese government announced its intention of phasing out FECs, but implementation seems to have been indefinitely postponed, and FECs remain in circulation.

FEC and Rmb may be reconverted into foreign currency or taken out when you leave China, but it is impossible to change them abroad.

Foreign Currency There is no limit to the amount of foreign currency you can bring into China. It is advisable to keep your exchange vouchers as the bank may demand to see them when you convert Chinese currency back into foreign currency on leaving China.

All the major freely negotiable currencies can be exchanged at the branches of the Bank of China, in hotels and stores.

Cheques and Credit Cards All the usual American, European and Japanese travellers cheques are acceptable. Credit cards are accepted in a limited number of Friendship Stores, hotels and banks. You should check with your credit card company or bank before you rely on this form of payment for your purchases. Personal cheques are sometimes taken in return for goods which are shipped after the cheque is cleared.

Tipping Tipping was forbidden in China, but is resurfacing with the recent announcement that, as an incentive to better service, tourism staff (including drivers and guides) are now officially allowed to accept bonuses and tips.

Travel Agencies

There are a number of State-owned corporations which handle foreign visitors to China, but the largest is China International Travel Service (CITS). Other large organizations providing similar services are China Travel Service (CTS) and China Youth Travel Service (CYTS).

CITS offers a comprehensive service covering accommodation, transport, food, sightseeing, interpreters and special visits to schools, hospitals, factories and other places foreigners might be interested to see. It also provides services such as ticket sales for walk-in customers (see Useful Addresses, page 124).

Holidays

In contrast to the long calendar of traditional Chinese festivals, modern China now has only three official holidays; May Day, 1 October (marking the founding of the People's Republic of China), and Chinese New Year, usually called the Spring Festival in China itself, which comes at the lunar new year.

Climate and Clothing

Xi'an's climate is much drier and cooler than that of southwest or southeast China, and less extreme than that of Beijing. In American terms the climate is similar to that of Wyoming. The Qinling Mountains to the south of the Wei River valley shield Xi'an from the southeastern monsoon, which brings much rain and considerable humidity to the neighbouring province of Sichuan. Annual precipitation is only 530–600 millimetres (21–4 inches). Most of the rainfall occurs in July, August and September.

Visitors arrive in large numbers from March onwards: many residents believe that spring is the best season, with the city at its most beautiful under clear, bright skies. Summer begins in May, and is usually fine and sunny. The hottest month is July when noon temperatures may reach 38°C (100°F). Late summer and early autumn is cooler and can be overcast. Late autumn is usually fine and winter is dry and cold with a little snow. At night during winter temperatures often drop below 0°C (32°F).

In mid-summer only the lightest clothing is necessary. In mid-winter thermal underwear and multi-layered clothing add to comfort.

Xi'an Temperatures

	Average	High	Low		Average	High	Low
Jan	−1.3°C (29°F)	5.1°C (41°F)	−5.5°C (22°F)	Jul	26.7°C (80°F)	34°C (93°F)	22.5°C (72°F)
Feb	2.1°C (36°F)	8°C (46°F)	−2.4°C (28°F)	Aug	25.4°C (78°F)	31.5°C (89°F)	20.9°C (70°F)
Mar	8°C (46°F)	14.7°C (58°F)	2.7°C (37°F)	Sept	19.4°C (67°F)	25°C (77°F)	15.5°C (60°F)
Apr	14°C (57°F)	21.5°C (70°F)	8.6°C (47°F)	Oct	13.6°C (57°F)	20°C (68°F)	8.9°C (48°F)
May	19.2°C (67°F)	27.7°C (82°F)	13.8°C (57°F)	Nov	6.5°C (44°F)	12.4°C (54°F)	2.3°C (36°F)
Jun	25.3°C (78°F)	32.8°C (91°F)	19°C (66°F)	Dec	0.6°C (33°F)	6.2°C (43°F)	−3.9°C (25°F)

Child's appliquéd vest featuring four of the 'five poisonous creatures'

Hotels

Xi'an did not have a Western-style hotel until the 1950s. In the early part of the century Chinese inns were open to foreigners, but many Western travellers arriving in Xi'an stayed with the European missionaries of the Scandinavian Alliance, the English Baptist Mission and the China Inland Mission.

When the rapid expansion of the tourist industry began in 1978, Xi'an was one of China's biggest tourist bottlenecks. However, the situation has now improved, and several new tourist hotels have already opened and older ones have been renovated. The city's first joint-venture hotel, the Golden Flower, opened in 1985 but the majority of the new international-standard hotels have yet to come. During 1988 and 1989 a flood of major new hotels run by international management chains are scheduled to open, and Xi'an will be better off than most provincial Chinese cities for quality accommodation.

As elsewhere in China, hotels in Xi'an offer a confusing array of room classes and prices. Facilities in the average hotels for foreigners — these are owned and run by Chinese authorities — usually include air conditioning and heating, a bank, telecommunications desk, and souvenir shops. Many now accept the better-known credit cards. Most hotels can organize sightseeing tours to the major sights. Rooms range from vast old-fashioned suites to modern, international-standard rooms. Standards of cleanliness and efficiency are equally varied.

Golden Flower Hotel (Jinhua Fandian)
Changle Xi Lu
tel. 32981
tlx. 70145, fax. 32327

金花饭店
长乐西路

205 rooms, US$105 (single), US$135 (double), US$250 (suite). From December to March attractive rates are available for two- and three-night packages inclusive of room, breakfast, airport shuttle and excursions. (Amex, Diners, Visa, MasterCard, JCB, Federal)

Opened in April 1985, this joint-venture hotel (Xi'an's first) is operated by SARA Hotels of Sweden to a high international standard. It is undoubtedly the best hotel in Xi'an. Staff are well-trained, helpful and friendly; between them they represent 11 countries and speak 15 different languages. Located just outside the eastern city wall, the Golden Flower's mirrored-glass exterior is a popular attraction for local people. Inside, the stylish atrium lobby astonishes visitors. The Western and Chinese restaurants, separated by a fountain, are recognized as among the best in China. The comfortable second-floor bar lounge offers live entertainment during the high season, and its adjoining small disco (open 8 pm—midnight and later at weekends) is one of Xi'an's few nightspots. The attractive rooms are amongst the largest of any of China's new hotels. The Western-style business centre (open 7 am—8 pm) handles secretarial work but, more important, makes flight reservations and train bookings on behalf of guests. Presently the hotel is expanding with an additional 300 rooms, an indoor/outdoor pool, health club, various restaurants and conference facilities.

Bell Tower Hotel (Zhonglou Fandian)
Southwest of the Bell Tower
tel. 22033, 24730
tlx. 70124, cable 8988

钟楼饭店
钟楼西南角

321 rooms, US$70—90 (single), US$80—95 (double), US$100—40 (suite)

This ideally located hotel, which first opened under local management in 1983, has been completely renovated by a Hong Kong group. It reopened under Holiday Inn management at the end of 1987, with revamped facilities (plus a new health club) and much-improved service. Western food is served in its Tower Café, and there is also a good Chinese restaurant. From the top floors there is an excellent view of the Bell Tower and the surrounding busy streets.

Xi'an Garden (Tanghua)
Xiaozhai Dong Lu

唐华饭店
小寨东路

301 rooms

Next to the Big Goose Pagoda, and set in expansive grounds, this Japanese-owned international-standard hotel is set to open in April 1988. The garden complex, which covers 100,000 square metres, will also contain a Tang Culture and Arts Museum, and the Tang Theatre Restaurant. The hotel restaurants will offer Western, Chinese and Japanese food. Health facilities and a shopping arcade are included in the plans.

Jianguo Hotel
Huzhu Lu

建国饭店
互助路

700 rooms, US$45 (single), US$60 (double), US$70 (super double)

This new highrise joint-venture hotel which has five restaurants, a pool, health centre, and large Friendship Store, is scheduled to open in August 1988. It is located just south of the Golden Flower, off Jianhua Bei Lu, close to the zoo. The overseas partner of the hotel also owns the Jianguo in Beijing, but the two hotels are run by different management groups.

Concord Hotel
12 Fenghao Lu
tel. 44829, 44529
cable 4460

协和饭店
丰镐路12号

166 rooms, US$55−65

This small hotel (a joint venture with a Hong Kong group) experienced some teething troubles when it first opened in 1986. But a new management is expected to take over, and service should improve. Its location, ten minutes' taxi-ride from the airport, is rather far out of town for easy sightseeing. Its rooms, which are on the small side, boast TV, plus in-house movies, and a mini-bar. There is a Western-style coffee shop, and a Chinese restaurant specializing in Sichuan cuisine.

People's Mansion (Renmin Dasha)
Dongxin Jie
tel. 715111

人民大厦
东新街

472 rooms, Rmb85−260 (double)

Recently renovated, this Chinese-run hotel with its imposing Soviet-style facade was originally built in the 1950s when it was occupied by Russian technical personnel. It now boasts 472 air-conditioned, heated rooms (most with telephones): 252 in the back building, and 220 in the front. A pleasant flower garden and fountain in the front courtyard make this part of the hotel especially attractive in the spring.

There are four dining rooms; the main one is in a separate east building, which also has a coffee shop and bar (open 8 am−12 pm). Another bar can be found on the third floor of the front building. Other facilities include souvenir shops and a games room. CITS and

CTS are both located in the back building.

Well-located in the centre of the city, the Renmin Dasha is within easy walking distance of Revolution Park to the north, and the shopping district of Nanxin Jie and Dong Dajie to the south. The Friendship Store is nearby on Nanxin Jie. Bicycles can be rented at the hotel gate for Rmb5 a day.

Xi'an Guesthouse
Chang'an Lu
tel. 51351

西安宾馆
长安路

500 rooms, Rmb100−240 (double)

Opened at the end of 1981, this 13-storey locally owned and managed hotel is a prominent Xi'an landmark. An additional building was completed in 1987. The hotel currently suffers from lackadaisical management, but discussions with a foreign management group are underway and service may improve. There are five dining rooms, offering Chinese, Western and Japanese food, and bars on the first and second floors that sell French, Italian and German wines, to the incongruous accompaniment of Cantonese and Japanese pop songs. On the top floor is a third bar (open only during summer) which is a pleasant spot for a relaxing drink.

Other facilities include an indoor pool, beauty parlour, film-developing studio and several good speciality shops including a carpet store with prices notably better than in Beijing.

The hotel commands a good view due north to the South Gate and the Bell Tower, and also southeast to the Big Goose Pagoda. The Little Goose Pagoda is only a short distance away.

Tangcheng Hotel
7 Lingyuan Nan Lu
tel. 54171, 55921
cable 3266

唐城饭店
陵园南路 7 号

400 rooms, Rmb120−280 (double)

Opened in 1986, this middle-range 14-storey hotel is located southwest of the city wall and is run by CITS who house many of their groups here. Its mediocre dining rooms feature a range of cuisines, from Sichuan and

Cantonese to Chinese-style Continental and American. Although the hotel has deteriorated rapidly, it does have some up-market luxuries, including IDD facilities and four-room suites with jacuzzi bathtubs.

Scarlet Bird Hotel (Zhujue Fandian)
Xiaozhai Xi Lu
tel. 53311

朱雀饭店
小寨西路

110 rooms, Rmb70−140 (double)

This is a spacious, three-storey, middle-range hotel which opened in 1985. In a slightly inconvenient location for sightseeing, it is southwest of the city wall, near the large Xiaozhai market. Its facilities include a banquet hall where both Western and Chinese food is served, a coffee shop, English-style bar and disco. At the back of the long, open lobby, works by local artists are for sale.

May the First Hotel (Wuyi Fandian)
Dong Dajie
tel. 718665

五一饭店
东大街

Rmb62

This is a modest, centrally located hotel, within easy walking distance of the Bell Tower Hotel, the Muslim quarter, several restaurants, the Friendship Store and other major stores. The decor is local taste, but it is clean and inexpensive. Rooms are heated and air-conditioned and have bathrooms. The hotel restaurant (open 8 am−10 pm) is a favoured place for banquets serving local cuisine.

Yulan Hotel
40 Changle Xi Lu
tel. 721519, 721414
tlx. 70016

榆兰饭店
长乐西路

70 rooms, Rmb30 (dormitory), Rmb100 (single/double), Rmb200 (suite)

Five minutes' walk west of the Golden Flower Hotel, this small hotel often handles its overspill in peak months. It is a standard Chinese owned and run hotel, although the staff are particularly friendly, and speak good English. Rooms have black-and-white TV.

Huaqing Guesthouse
Lintong Country

华清池宾馆
临潼县

30 beds, Rmb45

Although this small hotel is 30 kilometres (19 miles) outside Xi'an, it has a particularly attractive location, occupying the southwest corner of the Huaqing Palace Hot Springs, not far from the Mausoleum of the First Emperor of Qin and the Qin Terracotta Army Museum. The single-storey buildings are in Tang architectural style. A rather special feature is that hot spa water is piped into all the bathrooms.

Shaanxi Guesthouse
Zhangbagou
tel. 23831

陕西宾馆
丈八沟

178 rooms

Formerly for the exclusive use of high-ranking officials, foreign VIPs and diplomats, this expensive guesthouse occasionally accepts special tour groups but not usually walk-in guests. It is set in beautiful secluded gardens with a lake, close to the River Bi, about 17 kilometres (10.5 miles) southwest of the city centre. The guesthouse complex consists of ten two-storey residential buildings constructed in the 1950s. There are eight separate restaurants. Some of the suites are prodigiously large by international standards and can cost up to Rmb500 a night.

There are several other hotels in Xi'an that travellers on a low budget might try. The **Victory Hotel**, south of Heping Gate and close to the Provincial Song and Dance Theatre, is the best bet, with beds for Rmb11. **Jiefang Hotel**, across the square from the train station on the left, is a friendly, recently refurbished hotel, with very reasonable prices (Rmb25−75). Some restaurants on Dong Dajie such as the **Xi'an Restaurant** (tel. 719529) may also have rooms available.

Getting around Xi'an

There are some fascinating areas within the city walls which are well worth exploring on foot. Particularly interesting for their old buildings are the streets around the Drum Tower and the Great Mosque, as well as those near the North and East Gates and north and west of the Shaanxi Museum. Dong Dajie, the main shopping area, is another good place to stroll, with its large department stores and wide sidewalks. Xi Dajie is more compact and has dozens of small shops with a variety of intriguing items.

There are several trolleybus lines in the city and a number of bus lines, some of which extend into the newly developed urban areas (see map on pages 14—15). Public transport is cheap but can prove difficult unless you have full directions written out in Chinese or a basic knowledge of the language. Taxis are available at the hotels, and can also be hailed in the streets. There are usually taxis waiting at all the major places of interest to tourists. The drivers are supposed to charge by the kilometre travelled, but in practice they often charge a lump sum which is higher than the kilometre fee would be. It is best to establish the price before you set out, and to have your destinations written down in Chinese since taxi drivers rarely speak English.

If you prefer to cycle around Xi'an, you can rent a bicycle for Rmb5 a day from one of the numerous bicycle rental shops in the city centre. If you are near the People's Mansion, there is a conveniently located shop at the gate of the hotel (open 9 am—9 pm).

Many of Xi'an's major sights are a long way from the city. CITS arranges comfortable Japanese buses to transport tour groups to these places. Independent travellers can either take a taxi (and possibly hire a guide-interpreter from CITS) or, a much cheaper alternative, go on a day tour. These tours, in air-conditioned buses, include visits to the Qin Tomb and Terracotta Army, Banpo and Huaqing. They can easily be arranged at all major hotels for Rmb20—60 a day. One of the least expensive is available at the Renmin for Rmb30. Public buses also go to the Terracotta Army Museum, Huaqing Hot Springs, and to Banpo. They depart every half hour from a depot across the street from the railway station.

Shopping

Earlier this century Xi'an was known for its curio shops stocked with antiquities of the city. Today, however, you would be lucky to find anything very old; most antiques in these shops date from the Qing and Republican periods. Curio-hunters may well come across some genuine, though small, antiques in the shops at the major sights, notably the Terracotta Army Museum, the Qin Tomb, and Qian Ling Tombs. Enthusiastic salesmanship may win you over, but be wary of the centuries-old dates that are blithely tossed about and bargain hard. Xi'an's largest antique shop, the **Xi'an City Antique Store**, is handsomely housed inside the Drum Tower. It is worth visiting as much for its magnificent setting as its varied stock and reliable attributions.

Shaanxi's folk crafts are thriving with the rapid increase of tourism in Xi'an. Hawkers cluster round every site visited by tourists, selling brightly coloured patchwork waistcoats and shoulder bags, embroidered children's shoes, hats and toys, shadow puppets, and amusing painted clay ornaments decorated in brilliant primary colours. Buying in the free markets can be much more fun than in the established arts and crafts shops, but be prepared for some fierce bargaining. Prices should be considerably less than in the official stores. The **Shaanxi Folk Art Gallery**, 16 Yanta Lu (open 8.30 am−6.30 pm) accepts all the major credit cards, but sells little of real quality or interest.

*Fengxiang County
painted clay tiger*

Embroidery is one of Shaanxi's richest traditional skills that is gaining recognition elsewhere; some of the more distinctive items crop up in hotel souvenir shops and Friendship Stores in other parts of China. There are children's patchwork waistcoats, predominantly red, and decorated with some, or all, of the 'five poisonous creatures' — toad, snake, centipede, lizard, scorpion — in the belief that the process of sewing the forms onto the waistcoat will nullify the creatures' evil powers. Embroidered cylindrical cotton pillows, with an intricately decorated tiger's head at each end, are also common. These are favourite gifts to babies when the first month of life is celebrated. Tiger motifs often appear on other clothes and shoes for children, since the tiger can readily devour evil spirits. Its eyes are usually wide open and staring, to help deflect evil influences away from the wearer.

Painted clay toys, originally from the nearby city of Fengxiang, were traditional gifts for festivals, wedding and birthdays. But now they are available in many of the free markets and souvenir shops in the city, where they can be bought for a few *yuan*. These toys are often in the form of tigers, sometimes covered with flowers or butterflies, and predominantly red and green to symbolize prosperity and happiness. Other popular subjects are comical monkeys and chubby children.

Shadow puppets, cut out of semi-transparent hide and painted in bright colours, are another speciality of Xi'an. The puppet's flexible joints allow it — in skilled hands — to somersault expertly, or engage in armed combat. The characters depicted are usually from traditional folk tales.

Chinese stone rubbings are a very appropriate souvenir of China's former capital since Xi'an has the country's best collection of steles, or inscribed stone tablets, most of them in the Forest of Steles (see page 00). The rubbings of memorials, calligraphy, pictures and even maps, are produced by laying paper on top of a stele, and then pounding it with a tightly-wrapped ink-filled cloth formed into a kind of mallet. It is often possible to see this being done, either at the Forest of Steles or at a handicraft factory. An expert job from a famous stone can cost hundreds, even thousands, of *yuan*. Rubbings of all prices are on sale almost everywhere around the city.

You may find it interesting to visit the workshops and showrooms of some small handicraft enterprises. Quality varies; none of the factories is particularly old but some of the craft techniques are worth seeing, and you will always be given a warm welcome. The **Cloisonné Factory** of Xi'an which employs some 400 workers is at 21 Yanta Lu, near the Big Goose Pagoda. The **Jade Carving Factory** of Xi'an is at 173 Xiyi Lu, round the corner from the Friendship Store, and has a retail outlet. Some 250 workers carve jadeite, amethyst, crystal, many other semi-precious stones, and petrified wood. Attached to the factory is a unit making rubbings from reproductions of stones in the Forest of Steles. The **Xi'an Special Arts and Crafts Factory** on Huancheng Xi Lu, just north of the West Gate, makes sculptures and collage pictures using sea-shells, feathers, silk and other materials together with inlaid woodwork. There is another arts and crafts factory near the Big Goose Pagoda which opened in May 1981. This specializes in paintings and calligraphy, and miniature reproductions of the figures at the Qin Terracotta Army Museum.

Other interesting items found most easily at the small shops surrounding major sights include local pottery for everyday use, basketware, papercuts, and micro-carvings on pieces of ivory no bigger than a grain of rice.

The **Friendship Store,** obligatory stop on many CITS tours, is in Nanxin Jie (open 10 am−8 pm), and carries all the usual items found in Friendship Stores throughout China. But it also has a range of replicas of Xi'an's archaeological relics. There are Qin soldiers of varying sizes, but it is worth noting that you can buy these replicas for far less at the Terracotta Army Museum itself. A selection of Shaanxi handicrafts is worth looking at, along with works of Huxian peasant painters (see page 47) displayed on the second floor, and costumes worn by some of China's minority nationalities.

Replicas of Banpo pottery (see page 51) can be bought at the **Banpo Museum Retail Shop** (open 8 am−6 pm).

The main shopping street is Dong Dajie, particularly the section between Nanxin Jie and the Bell Tower. The principal department store, the **Dong Dajie Department Store**, is located on the south side of Dong Dajie on the corner of Luoma Shi, a small alley. Carrying the most up-to-date products available to local Xi'an people, it is interesting to visit even if you do not plan to buy anything. The **Overseas Chinese Department Store,** which sells a range of everyday goods including clothing, is on the corner of Nanxin Jie, right next to the Friendship Store.

Further along Dong Dajie are the **Foreign Languages Bookshop**, **Xinhua Bookshop** (for publications in Chinese), and shops selling posters, clocks, sunglasses and an assortment of other products. There are also restaurants, snack-bars and fruit and vegetable stalls.

Just round the corner, and opposite the Bell Tower, is a **Chinese opera costume shop** (at 488 Dongfeng Lu), supplying the municipal and county opera troupes of Shaanxi Province with embroidered silk costumes, elaborate head-dresses, hats, false beards and whiskers and odd props.

An excellent art store, called the **Chang'an Calligraphy and Painting Store**, can be found just off Xi Dajie, on the street that leads you through the Drum Tower. The shop has good quality paintings, calligraphy, brushes, ink-stones, name-chops, paper, etc.

Another important shopping area is around Jiefang Lu, in the northeast of the walled city. There are two department stores here, the **Jiefang Lu** and the **Minsheng.** Markets selling everyday goods can be found in the area round the Bell Tower or clustered round the East, South, or North Gates.

Oriental carpets from the western provinces of Xinjiang and Gansu, traditionally called Chinese Turkestan, are best found in hotel shops, notably the **Xi'an Guesthouse**. Prices are better here than in the larger Chinese cities like Beijing and Shanghai.

Food and Drink

In Xi'an the fare is generally plain and provincial, although good food is available if you search it out. Street-stall cooking is often better than that offered by the restaurants, which is itself usually better than the convenient but unexciting meals served by the hotels.

In country areas of Shaanxi Province (of which Xi'an is the capital) noodles and steamed bread are more popular than rice, and mutton is an important source of protein. Eating habits throughout the northwest of China have been strongly influenced by the *Hui*, Chinese-speaking Muslims who of course do not eat pork. Their food can be sampled at the stalls around the Drum Tower, especially in the early evening. The best-known, best-loved dish is called *kaoyangrou*, spicy barbecued mutton on skewers. Boiled mutton ravioli served in spicy sauce, *yangrou shuijiao*, sold by the bowl for a few *mao*, can be found in the same area.

The most popular local dish, also *Hui* in origin, is the hearty *yangrou paomo*. For the standard local price of about Rmb1, a large bowl and two large baked flatbreads are provided. The customer breaks the bread into very small pieces and takes the bowl back to the kitchen, where a mutton and vegetable soup, with noodles, is poured over the broken pieces of bread. It is difficult to describe the taste — perhaps something like haggis stew, noodles and digestive biscuits comes closest to it!

At a relatively more sophisticated level, Xi'an has its own special delicacies served in some of the larger restaurants. Banquets start with a cold plate of *hors d'oeuvres* arranged in the shape of a phoenix, peacock or butterfly. Other dishes include fish in milk soup, served in a copper chafing dish (*guozi yu*), coin-shaped egg and hair vegetable (*jinqian facai*), sliced pig tripe and duck gizzard (*cuan shuang cui*), whole, crispy 'calabash' chicken (*hulu ji*), and braised quail (*tiepa anchun*). Chinese wolfberry and white fungus in soup (*gouqi dun yiner*) is a tonic, particularly good for the lungs.

Sweet dishes offered in ordinary eating establishments tend to be sugary, starchy and filled with red bean, peanuts or *baihe*, lily bulb. A number of different cakes and biscuits are on sale, including crystal cakes (*shuijing bing*) and egg-thread cakes (*dansi bing*).

The leading brand of liquor is called *Xifeng*, a colourless spirit made in Liulin Village, near Fengxiang about 145 kilometres (90 miles) west of Xi'an. Another local drink is the Yellow Osmanthus Thick Wine (*Huanggui choujiu*). Both are said to owe their origin to alcoholic drinks of the Tang period. Xi'an has a few varieties of its own beer, the best of which is aptly named 'Xian Beer'.

Restaurants in Xi'an are generally open from around 11 am to 7 pm — but note that many restaurants will not serve guests without reservations after 6 pm. The standard charge for an ordinary meal for a foreigner is around Rmb15 per person. Banquets are two or three times that figure.

Restaurants

**Jufengyuan
Restaurant**
Jiefang Lu
tel. 24736

聚丰园
解放路

Formerly called the Xi'an Sichuan Restaurant, this restaurant serves authentic Sichuanese food, which is characteristically hot and spicy. Their 'Pock-marked Grandma Chen's Beancurd' (*mapo doufu*), named after the lady who invented it, eel in garlic sauce (*dasuan shanyu*) and chicken diced with chilli (*mala jiding*), are excellent.

**May the First
Restaurant
(Wuyi Fandian)**
Dong Dajie
tel. 718665

五一饭店
东大街

This downtown hotel restaurant is popular for banquets and provides local-style food. The staff is efficient and service is prompt but prices are high by Xi'an standards. Roast chicken with 'five-spice' is a particularly delicious dish on the menu. It is open 8 am– 10 pm.

**Peace Restaurant
(Heping Fandian)**
Dachashi
tel. 714726

和平饭店
大差市

This relatively expensive restaurant caters almost exclusively to foreign tour groups and provides a variety of local dishes adapted to international tastes. It is not the place to experience local food or atmosphere. Various hotpot dishes, including lamb or mushrooms with rice noodles, may be included in the banquet menu. Sugared pork-fat, a Chinese favourite, is served here. It opens at 9.30 am and closes late.

Xi'an Restaurant
Intersection of Dong Dajie and Juhuayuan
tel. 719529

西安饭店
东大街菊花园口

The largest restaurant of the city occupies a huge modern block with six floors containing 14 dining rooms. There is little discernible ambience. Food is officially Shaanxi-style, and many of the delicacies, such as *kaoyangrou* and *yangrou shuijiao*, are available; however, the chefs are flexible and can cook other kinds of Chinese cuisine. The calligraphy of the sign in front of the building is by Guo Moruo, a literary eminence of the People's Republic.

**East Asia Restaurant
(Dongya Fandian)**
Luoma Shi
tel. 719492

东亚饭店
骡马市

All the chefs in this restaurant, which is near
the Bell Tower, were originally from
Shanghai, and officially they prepare the
cuisine of Suzhou and Wuxi, cities in southern
Jiangsu Province, close to Shanghai. In
practice most of the food is local in style.
They serve their own 'East Asia' hotpot
(*dongya huoguo*), a close relative of the
Mongolian hotpot. Other dishes which might
be tried include 'snow pagoda white fungus'
(*xueta yiner*), 'quadruple treasures beancurd'
(*sibao doufu*) and an almond blancmange
(*xingren doufu*).

**Baiyunzhang Beef
and Mutton Ravioli
House**
Intersection of Dong
Dajie and Juhuayuan
tel. 719247

白云章牛羊肉饺子馆
东大街菊花园口

Located very close to the Xi'an Restaurant,
this is the place to try one of the most
celebrated ordinary dishes of north China,
jiaozi, whose nearest Western equivalent is
the Italian ravioli. *Jiaozi* can be prepared and
cooked in a number of different ways but
essentially are made of hard-wheat pasta filled
with chopped meat and vegetable.

Qingya Restaurant
Dong Dajie

清雅饭馆
东大街

This is a Muslim restaurant which is run
entirely by *Hui*, or Chinese Muslims. They
specialize in lamb and vegetable dishes.
Especially good are their lamb *jiaozi*. It is on
the south side of Dong Dajie, a little west of
the Dong Dajie Department Store going
towards the Bell Tower.

New China Snacks
Dong Dajie

新中华
东大街

Between the Dong Dajie Department Store
and the Qingya Restaurant (see above), on
the south side of the road, is a small but
typical sweet snack shop. Everything is very
cheap and the only way to order is to point.
Fried glutinous rice, covered with sugar and
containing red bean, is one favourite. Another
is sweet congee, rice gruel in syrup with
peanuts or *baihe*, lily bulb.

**Jiefanglu Jiaozi
Restaurant**
Jiefang Lu
tel. 23185

解放路饺子馆
解放路

Located near the railway station, this is one of the best restaurants in town and is always packed with customers. It is advisable to book in advance. The total repertoire of the restaurant includes 125 varieties of dumpling (*jiaozi*) and other speciality dishes which can be cooked on request.

A standard meal begins with excellent varied *hors d'oeuvres* which are then followed by 16 different varieties of dumpling. Some are fried and some are steamed; all are freshly cooked, and go under exotic names such as 'Buddha's claw', 'concubine's dumpling' and 'make-money'. If you eat there on another day, you may sample another 16 flavours.

Dumpling meals are rounded off with a delicious chicken and duck 'dragon soup' served in a bubbling brass tureen over a burner, with miniature dumplings cooked in it at the table. There are more bowls of dumplings for anyone who is still hungry.

**Tongdexiang Niu
Yangrou Paomo
House**
Shehui Lu entrance
tel. 22170

同德祥牛羊肉泡馍馆
社会路口

A *paomo* and mutton hotpot banquet at this unpretentious restaurant is excellent value and is one of the most authentically Chinese experiences in town. On the edge of the Bell Tower Muslim quarter, the restaurant is well patronized by locals. The banquet menu includes varied *hors d'oeuvres* and traditional *paomo* (dry starchy bread broken into small pieces and submerged in hot, lightly spiced mutton broth), but the most highly recommended dish is the Mongolian-style hotpot cooked at the table. You hold the thinly sliced raw meat with chopsticks in the boiling water of the hotpot to cook it for a few seconds, then flavour it with a variety of sauces. This is followed by 'dragon's moustache' soup, made with long rice noodles and vegetables. The restaurant is open 9 am−7 pm.

**Jade Spring and Wan
Fu Court**
Golden Flower Hotel
Changle Xi Lu
tel. 32981

玉泉轩
万福阁
金花饭店
长乐西路

To date the Jade Spring has been the only
restaurant in Xi'an preparing Continental
cuisine, although more will open in the new
international hotels over the next few years.
The menu offers an interesting range of
appetizers, including Norwegian smoked
salmon (Rmb30), soups, salads, and grills
(Rmb28−65), as well as a few Swedish dishes
(the hotel is run by SARA, a Swedish
management group). There is a mouth-
watering pastry wagon, and a good wine list.
You can take a light lunch here — a single
spaghetti course or sandwiches or try the set
lunch menu which is good value at Rmb40.
This is one of the few places in the city where
you can linger over an *à la carte* dinner in the
evening. The Jade Spring starts its breakfast
buffet at 6 am, and the restaurant stays open
until 11 pm.

On the opposite side of Golden Flower's
large dining area is the Chinese restaurant,
Wan Fu Court, which offers the best Chinese
food in Xi'an. Its wide-ranging menu includes
a number of modified Sichuan dishes, as well
as Cantonese cuisine. There is a separate
seafood menu. Wan Fu Court is open 11.30
am−2.30 pm, and 6−10 pm.

**Tangcheng Hotel
Western Restaurant**
7 Lingyuan Nan Lu
tel. 54171, 55921

唐城饭店西餐厅
陵园南路 7 号

For those who would like a change from
Chinese cuisine, the Tangcheng serves a
limited range of Western-style food. Its
Western Restaurant, open all day, serves full
three-course meals and snacks. Main courses
include steak and sole *meunière*. The snacks
are highly recommended, especially the
generous servings of French toast, with plenty
of butter and honey. The club sandwiches are
also tasty and filling.

Entertainment and the Arts

Xi'an is the home of a number of professional performing arts organizations, serving both the city and the Shaanxi countryside. The city also has its own Conservatory of Music (at Daxingshan Temple Park), a provincial Opera School attached to the Institute of Opera in Wenyi Lu, and its own film studio (see page 119) near the Big Goose Pagoda.

The **Shaanxi Acrobatics Troupe**, which includes conjurors, is very popular with local people. Together with most of the various performing arts groups, this is based near Wenyi Lu, just south of the walled city. Close by is the building of the **Shaanxi Song and Dance Troupe**. This company is known for its vocal, orchestral and instrumental performances of both Chinese and Western music, including Western light classical, international folk and Chinese operatic pieces.

The **Xi'an Song and Dance Troupe** concentrates on Western ballet and Chinese traditional dance. Like the Shaanxi troupe it has its own orchestra. It is also located south of the walled city, at a small studio near Xiaozhai, although it performs in many different places. Xi'an also has the **Shaanxi Puppet Group**, and a troupe specializing in Chinese traditional story-telling and comic dialogues.

There are eight big theatres in the city. The most important is the **People's Theatre** on Bei Dajie. This is mainly used for concerts, dancing and Beijing opera (performed by the Shaanxi Number One and Shaanxi Number Two Opera Companies).

If you have time to see only one artistic performance you should perhaps choose the celebrated local Qinqiang opera of Shaanxi Province itself.

China has over 300 forms of local theatre, and Qinqiang is one of the oldest, most vigorous and most influential of them all. It is almost certainly the original form of 'clapper' opera, with which it is synonymous. In this style of Chinese opera, popular today throughout much of northern China, time is beaten with large wooden clap boards that look like oversized castanets.

Xi'an city has two Qinqiang companies. The drama is performed in local Xi'an dialect, with its own characteristic, rather loud, vocal style, accompanied by string instruments. It has its own conventions of costume and make-up. Individual operas are often three or four hours long with rapidly developed plots using all the dramatic devices found in Shakespearian comedies — abrupt changes in fortune, mistaken identities, men dressed as women, women dressed as men, both as animals (notably predatory, acrobatic tigers). Drag parts in which comedians take off vulgar, meddlesome old ladies are often star roles.

Despite its stylization, Chinese opera is a spectacular and dramatic spectacle. However, foreigners and Chinese who do not understand the local dialect would benefit from having read an outline of the story before arriving at the theatre. Performances are advertized in the local newspapers, the *Xi'an Daily* and the *Shaanxi Daily*. Tickets can be purchased at the theatre and sometimes at major hotels. The People's Mansion (Renmin Dasha) has its own theatre where there are regular performances of recreated Tang-style dances during the summer season.

Flora and Fauna

During the Tang Dynasty (618−907) horticulture flourished in the capital Chang'an (present-day Xi'an). One of its citizens was the most celebrated gardener of Chinese history, the hunchback 'Camel' Guo. He is supposed to have grown golden peaches and propagated lotus with deep blue flowers by soaking the seeds in indigo dye.

The inhabitants of the capital were especially proud of their tree peonies, which became something of a mania, and blooms were sold for huge sums in the Chang'an Flower Market. The most popular colours were pale pink and deep purple. Tree peonies had been cultivated from about the fifth century onwards, originally in either Shaanxi or Sichuan. (The plant did not reach Europe until 1789 when the first one was found a home in London's Kew Gardens.) The best peony garden was at Da Cien Temple, the temple of the Big Goose Pagoda (see page 89). It is no longer there today, but the **Xi'an Botanical Garden** (open every day 10 am−6 pm) has a small garden and is an excellent place to escape the crowds that fill most tourist sights. It is located on Hua Lu, south of the city, and can be reached by bus number 5 or by taxi.

In the second century BC, an envoy of Emperor Han Wudi (reigned 140−86 BC), who was sent to central Asia, brought the pomegranate tree back to China. Today, during the months of May and June, the hillsides around Lintong County, including the slopes of the Mausoleum of the First Emperor of Qin, are covered with the red and white flowers of the pomegranate. The fruit grown in Xi'an and especially Lintong, 15 kilometres (9 miles) to the east, is considered the best in the country, giving rise to the Chinese saying that 'When you think of Lintong, you think of pomegranates'.

The first attempt to catalogue the animals, birds and reptiles of Shaanxi according to Western science was made in 1908−9. Robert Stirling Clark of New York led an expedition of 36 men, including the ornithologist Arthur de C. Sowerby of the Smithsonian.

Among some of today's rarest birds that Sowerby recorded seeing were the pink, grey and white 'Chinese' ibises. These wading birds, members of the stork family, are properly called Japanese ibis, though they are called *toki* in Japan. The long-beaked birds are distinguished by the bright red colouring of the side of the head and of the legs. The adult grows to a length of about 77 centimetres (2.5 feet) head to tail.

These ibises were formerly spread throughout east and northeast China, Korea and Japan, but apparently environmental changes in the 20th century were disastrous for the species. They declined in numbers and disappeared altogether after 1964. By 1980 there were only two known pairs left in the world. These were at the Toki Protection

Centre on Japan's Sado Island. They had not reproduced for four years, and artificial incubation had failed. Then, that same year, Chinese zoologists found two nesting pairs in Shaanxi, at Yangxian County in the Qinling Mountains. Three young were hatched that year in what is now the Qinling Number One Ibis Colony.

By comparison with the ibis, the giant panda is not nearly so rare. There are still about 1,000 of these large black and white, high-altitude living, bamboo-munching 'cat-bears'. Most of them are in the neighbouring province of Sichuan; a few unlucky, if pampered, ones play star roles in world zoos. In Shaanxi Province there is one special nature reserve for them at Foping County, southwest of Xi'an and not far from the Qinling Ibis Colony.

The orange snub-nosed monkey, also known as the golden-haired monkey, is another inhabitant of the Qinling Mountains. Found in birch forests and mountain gullies, at around 2,500−3,000 metres (8,000−10,000 feet), these very agile acrobatic animals have bright yellow-orange fur, with white chests, long tails and distinctive blue circles around their eyes.

The so-called Reeves's pheasant is the original proud possessor of the long, waving tail feathers worn by generals in Chinese opera. The tail of the male reaches to 100−40 centimetres (3.5−4.5 feet) long. The bird is found in mountain forests, between 600−2,000 metres (2,000−6,500 feet) above sea level.

The **Xi'an Zoo** in Jinhua Bei Lu (tel. 31502) has examples of both giant and lesser pandas, pheasants and orange snub-nosed monkeys as well as northeast China tigers, leopards, Sichuan parrots, wild donkeys and other animals indigenous to China. There are also a number of animals presented to the Xi'an Zoo by the Japanese cities of Kyoto and Nara, with which Xi'an has a formal as well as an historical relationship. The zoo was established in Revolution Park in 1956, but moved to a much larger site to the east in 1976.

Until surveys are published of the complete fauna of southern Shaanxi we will not have a definitive inventory of species. The British traveller, Violet Cressy-Marcks, who interviewed Mao Zedong in Yan'an, recorded in 1938 that in an area 20 miles from the city she saw 'common jay, Chinese jay, blue magpie, golden eagle, pheasants, green woodpeckers, flocks of bustard, wild horned sheep and wild ducks and I was told there were leopards but I did not see any.' Near Xi'an 'there were many sulphur bellied rats, wood and field mice, also mallard, teal, wrens, redstarts, minks and goral.' At Lintong she saw 'geese, ducks, hares, snipe, bustard and mallard'. The wildlife of the Wei River plain is almost certainly much depleted now, in contrast to that of the mountains to the south.

The Peasant Painters of Huxian

In 1958, a group of farmers in Huxian, a county some 40 kilometres (25 miles) outside Xi'an, did some paintings to record progress on the construction of a new reservoir. So successful were the paintings that they inspired the organization of special painting centres to help the peasants develop their art. By the mid-1970s, there were about 2,000 active painters in the county, all of them farmers who would bicycle to the centres after a hard day's work in the fields. These centres are still the support system for Huxian's peasant artists. Painting materials, and a certain amount of professional guidance, are given, but the basic technical tuition does not seem to have squashed the creative independence of the better painters of the Group.

The distinctive style developed by the Huxian painters has won them national, and international, recognition. Exhibitions have already been held in Hong Kong, Sweden, London, the U.S. and Canada, as well as in Beijing and Shanghai.

The paintings are a complete contrast from the misty landscapes and muted colour of classic Chinese watercolours. The work of the peasants of Huxian is humorous, vibrant, dependent on brilliant colour, and intricate surface pattern, sometimes with a total disregard for perspective. Something of the intricate design of local embroidery is carried through to the paintings.

Themes chosen reflect the painters' everyday life as farmers — drying fish, feeding chicks, reeling silk, wedding parties and other festivities. Some painters record, with an almost childlike accuracy of observation, change within their society — horses hauling carts of concrete, for example, or a confrontation between an ox-drawn cart and a tractor. Legend and traditional opera stories are also a rich source of themes for the painters.

The Group claims that over 100,000 paintings have already been produced. Some 200 paintings are on display in eight rooms at the modest Huxian Peasant Painting Exhibition Hall, about one-and-a-half hours taxi-ride from Xi'an.

Visitors to Xi'an will find a small selection of paintings on sale at the Friendship Store. But top quality work from the most creative artists of the Group is more difficult to come by, and much more expensive. The work of Wang Jinglong, an orchard farmer, for instance, which is strikingly different from most of the Group, has already aroused worldwide interest on account of its strong individual interpretation of everyday happenings. Lou Zhijin and Liu Fengtao are two other names to look for.

Pictures (following pages) are reproduced courtesy of the Alvin Gallery, Hong Kong, which has been responsible for exhibiting some of the best work of the Huxian painters.

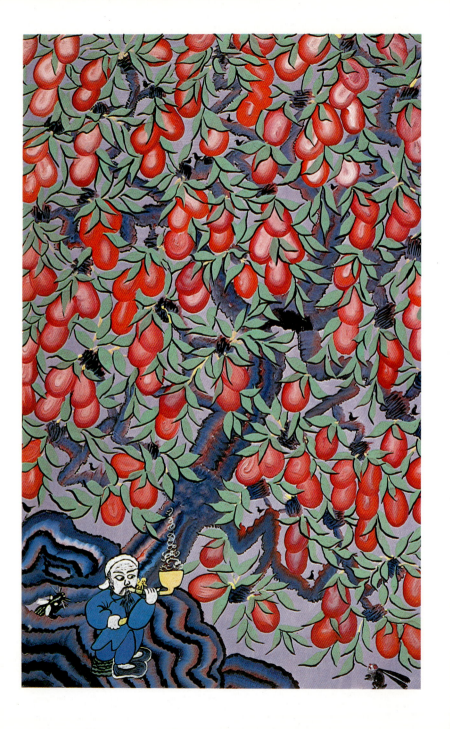

Huxian paintings by Wang Jinglong:
(facing page)
'Abundant Fruit',
(right)
'Family Plots in the Countryside', and
(below)
'Pulling Concrete'

Places of Interest in the Xi'an Area

Period One: Pre-Qin

Background

Xi'an lies a few miles south of the Wei River, a western tributary of
the Yellow River. Near the modern city is the ancient site of Chang'an
(Everlasting Peace), which served as the capital of several ruling
dynasties spanning a period of over 1,000 years. But the Wei valley
had been settled much earlier. In fact, both the Wei valley and Shaanxi
Province are traditionally known as the 'cradle' of Chinese civilization.
The Yellow Emperor — the mythical ancestor and first sovereign of
the Han race who is said to have lived in the third millennium BC —
has his legendary burial place at Huangling, a town halfway between
Xi'an and Yan'an in northern Shaanxi.

Palaeolithic Before the present landscape of the Wei valley was
created from deposits of sand blown from the Mongolian Plateau, early
ancestors of man lived in the area. During 1963−6 a skull (now in
Beijing), jaw and various other bones of Lantian Man, a form of
Homo erectus dating to around 800,000 BC, were discovered 38
kilometres (27 miles) southeast of Xi'an.

In the spring of 1978 another startling discovery was made: an
almost complete skull of what is now known as Dali Man in Dali
County, near the provincial border with Shanxi. He is thought to
belong to an early subspecies of *Homo sapiens*, living in perhaps
300,000 or 200,000 BC.

Neolithic The development of agriculture found an ideal setting in
the Wei and middle Yellow River valleys, with their deep loess deposit
containing all the necessary minerals for successful cultivation. From
approximately 5000 BC onwards settlements were formed, larger and
more permanent than similar ones elsewhere in the world. The early
Neolithic stage in China is called the Yangshao Culture. The name
Painted Pottery Culture is sometimes preferred, which contrasts with
the Black Pottery, or Longshan, Culture which followed it. Yangshao
Culture lasted until around 3000 BC. A typical Yangshao or Painted
Pottery Culture settlement has been excavated at Banpo, on the
outskirts of Xi'an.

Sights

Banpo Museum

In 1953 when workers were laying foundations for a factory at Banpo, less than seven kilometres (five miles) east of Xi'an, they came upon the remains of an ancient settlement. The discovery of this New Stone Age village has been described as the 'greatest single contribution to prehistoric archaeology in east Asia' (John Hay, *Ancient China*). Dating from approximately 5000 to 4000 BC, it is the most complete example of an agricultural Neolithic settlement anywhere in the world. Its remarkably well-preserved condition makes it a major attraction for visitors to Xi'an.

An area of 4,000 square metres (one acre) has been fully excavated, enclosed and put on view to the public. Foundations of 45 houses have been uncovered, some round, some square. The largest dwelling may have been a communal meeting place, or alternatively the house of the chief. Among the other impressive finds are: 200 storage pots, a collection of pottery and tools, a pottery-making centre and a graveyard with more than 250 graves.

The museum is simply but sensibly laid out. The main hall, in the rear, was built over the excavation site. Two smaller exhibition halls by the entrance display unearthed items, drawings and explanatory notes in both Chinese and English.

From the implements and utensils unearthed, archaeologists have learned a great deal about the daily life of Banpo. It was a typical Yangshao Culture community. Between 200–300 people lived there, practising slash-and-burn agriculture. They depended on millet and pork for their existence. In addition to millet, they planted vegetables such as cabbage and mustard, and hemp which was used to make clothing. They kept pigs, dogs and perhaps chickens and other animals. They also hunted and fished. They fired and painted extra-ordinarily beautiful red clay pots with both abstract and non-abstract designs. The earlier decorations on these vessels portrayed fish with mouths open, fishnets and deer on the run — subjects reflecting the main preoccupations of Banpo's inhabitants. Gradually, as the

displayed pots show quite clearly, the designs became abstract: the fish
motif, for instance, was later replaced by a geometric pattern.

Chinese archaeologists believe that a primitive communist
matriarchal clan lived at Banpo. In the communal burial ground found
to the north of the site, men and women were buried separately,
usually by themselves, sometimes in multiple single-sex graves.
Women were generally interred with a greater number of funeral
objects than men. However, it has been pointed out by foreign
archaeologists that in most early matriarchal settlements, excavated
elsewhere, whole families related through the female line have been
found buried together.

The Banpo Museum is located at the eastern end of the city, a
convenient stop on the way to or from the Terracotta Warriors. It can
be reached by bus number 8 from the Bell Tower or trolleybus number
5 from Dongwu Lu. It is open every day 9 am−5.30 pm.

Remains of the Capitals of the Western Zhou

Bronze metallurgy was practised from about the middle of the millennium, contemporary with the emergence of the Shang Dynasty. During
this period (1600−1027 BC), the Wei and Jing valleys were dominated
by a relatively backward people called the Zhou. Under their leader,
King Wu, they attacked and captured Anyang, the capital of the
Shang, in 1027 BC. The Zhou Dynasty lasted formally until 249 BC,
but the kings only enjoyed real power until 771 BC. This period is
called the Western Zhou. Archaeologists have discovered the remains
of two Zhou palaces west of Xi'an, at Fengchu Village, Qishan
County, and at Zhaochen Village, Fufeng County.

A **Western Zhou chariot burial pit** was unearthed at **Zhangjiapo**,
Chang'an County, in 1955. The war chariot was the pre-eminent
symbol of power in the Bronze Age. One of the pits excavated at
Zhangjiapo contained two chariots and the remains of six horses and

one slave, interred as part of the funeral of a lord. These are on display in a small museum west of the city, near Dou Men village, and accessible by taxi.

It is recorded that the Zhou established five different capitals in the Wei and Jing valleys at different times. Two of these have been identified. **Fengjing** on the western bank of the Feng River was an early capital. **Haojing** on the opposite bank was the capital from 1027 to 771 BC. The sites have been excavated and the remains of houses, workshops, burials and some hoards of bronze articles have been found and removed to the Xianyang and Shaanxi Provincial Museums. Nothing of the old capitals can now be seen at the original sites.

Western Zhou-Dynasty
bronze incense burner

Period Two: The Qin Empire

Background

The Rise of Qin The Eastern Zhou began with the re-establishment of the capital near Luoyang, Henan Province, in 770 BC. The dynasty is divided into two periods, the Spring and Autumn Annals (770–476 BC) and the Warring States (475–221 BC), both taken from the names of books. During the former the Zhou kings were only nominal leaders and the Chinese world was divided into more than 100 petty principalities; by the beginning of the latter, these had been absorbed into seven much larger states.

The Warring States period saw the beginning of the Iron Age in China, a time of tremendous technological progress in the arts of both war and peace. In due course Qin (Ch'in) — based near modern Xi'an — became the most powerful of the contending states, and flourished as the result of a single-minded emphasis on military prowess, public works and food production.

The First Emperor In 246 BC King Zheng came to the Qin throne, a mere boy of 13. During his reign Qin superiority was finally established when the six other states were annexed between 230 and 221 BC, unifying China for the first time ever.

King Zheng took the title of Qin Shihuangdi, First Emperor of Qin. (The term *huangdi* had previously only been used for deities and mythological hero-rulers such as the Yellow Emperor. *Qin* itself is the origin of our word 'China'.) His capital was at Xianyang (see page 60), northeast of the present-day town, on the north bank of the Wei River.

An emperor of vast ambitions and achievements, Qin Shihuangdi had a profound influence on Chinese history and culture, both in his life and death. The colossal scale and careful detail of his army of terracotta warriors (see below) shows beyond any doubt the advanced state of artistic and technological development of ancient Chinese culture, which historians in China have always claimed.

The great clay army is certainly also a fitting memorial to the man who first really united what were until then disparate states of China. Qin Shihuangdi, who has been called both tyrant and reformer, ruled over a vast territory. Having gained predominance over the various ruling houses, he became the sole source of power and final authority for a centralised government in Xianyang. To consolidate his huge empire, he introduced several important reforms: he personally supervised the organization of a uniform Chinese written language and prescribed 100 officially approved surnames for all his subjects.

The First Emperor's government was severe. He administered a strict legal code, whereby a whole family would be executed for the crimes of one of its members; he taxed the people and conscripted millions of labourers for both military and civil projects. To safeguard the northern frontier, the existing defensive lines along the border were rebuilt and extended to become China's Great Wall. Armies were sent as far south as today's Vietnam. Roads, irrigation schemes, palaces and above all his mausoleum all required hordes of reluctant labourers. Out of a total population of 20 million, one and a half million are thought to have been called to some form of service to the State. At the same time, independent thought was suppressed: books whose contents were considered subversive were burned, and hundreds of scholars were buried alive. These oppressive policies caused suffering on a huge scale, and on Qin Shihuangdi's death revolts swiftly followed.

Sights

Qin Terracotta Army Museum

One of the major sites of interest in China, this is an archaeological find of monumental scale. Literally an army of sculptured warriors — no two exactly alike — it is a stunning display that every visitor to China should see.

The discovery of the terracotta soldiers was like a legend come true for the villagers living in the area. For centuries they had been telling stories about the ghosts who lived underground and who were unearthed wherever they dug. Then, during a drought in the spring of 1974, some farmers decided to sink a well at a spot less than one and a half kilometres (less than a mile) east of the First Emperor's Mausoleum. This happened to be exactly at right angles to the centre of the original outer enclosure. As the farmers dug, they came upon (in the words of *Newsweek*), 'the clay clones of an 8,000-man army'.

When the first figures were unearthed, it was not appreciated how many there were, but gradually the significance of the discovery was realized: the emperor had decided to take an army with him to the nether world.

Whether he meant actually to move the whole army nearer to his own tomb, or to make this place the warriors' permanent resting place, is still not known. Some archaeologists think this could have been merely a storage place for the figures. But excavations are still being carried out, albeit at a painstakingly slow pace, and new discoveries may continue to be unearthed for many years to come.

The Qin Terracotta Army Museum, which opened in 1979, is a large hangar-like building constructed over Pit Number One, the place of the original discovery in 1974. There are two exhibition halls outside the main building, in which are displayed bronze chariots (see below) and an assortment of pottery figures and horses (touched up in what are believed to be the original colours) and weapons.

The terracotta figures were found in a vault five metres (16 feet) below the surface. The vault was originally built with walls of pounded earth, and a wooden roof was added before the enclosure was sealed. It appears that the troops of General Xiang Yu, who had already plundered the nearby imperial tomb, Qin Ling, opened the vault in 206 BC and set fire to the roof, which collapsed, smashing the terracottas *in situ*, and preserving them in mud and ash.

Terracotta Troops The terracotta soldiers are remarkably realistic pieces of sculpture. Each soldier's face has individual features, prompting speculation that they were modelled from life. They have squarish faces with broad foreheads and large, thick-lipped mouths, and they wear neat moustaches, and sometimes beards. Some of them have their hair in a topknot. Expressions are generally austere, eyes focused far ahead. The figures are mostly 1.8 metres (5 feet 11 inches) in height. The lower part of the body is solid, the upper hollow. They were originally painted, but the colour has been almost entirely lost.

The soldiers are divided into infantry armed with swords and spears, archers, crossbow archers, cavalry, chariot drivers and officers. The chariots no longer exist except for their metal fittings. They were almost certainly real ones, made of wood. Each is drawn by four pottery horses, on average 1.5 metres (4 feet 11 inches) tall by 2 metres (6 feet 7 inches) long.

The terracotta troops bear real arms, made of bronze. A huge number has been unearthed: swords, daggers, billhooks, spears, halberds, axes, crossbow triggers and arrowheads. The copper-tin alloy used was combined with 11 other elements such as nickel, magnesium, cobalt and chrome, and many weapons have emerged sharp, shiny and untarnished. The arrow-heads contain a poisonous percentage of lead.

The Excavations Pit Number One has 11 parallel corridors running from east to west, between larger open spaces at either end. The vault is estimated to cover a total area of 12,000 square metres (14,350 square yards), of which 2,000 square metres (2,390 square yards) have been excavated. So far 1,087 warriors, remains of eight wooden chariots, two bronze chariots and 32 terracotta horses have been unearthed. The excavated soldiers face east in battle formation. Three rows, each of 70 lightly-armed archers, form the vanguard. They are

followed by 38 columns of more heavily-armed infantry interspersed with war chariots. A single column of spearmen face north, south and west respectively. From the evidence of test excavations it is thought that there may be more than 8,000 pieces of pottery in total. A raised walkway round three sides of the vault allows visitors to view the soldiers from several angles. The spot where the discovery was first made is marked.

An L-shaped vault, now called Pit Number Two, was found north-east of Number One in May 1976. It contained nearly 1,000 terracotta pieces, including four chariots, cavalrymen leading their mounts, crossbow archers and foot soldiers. One figure, 1.95 metres (6 feet 5 inches) in height, is considered to be a general and commander of the charioteers. He wears an engraved armour and would have held a sword in his left hand. A number of figures were removed before the vault was refilled with earth.

Another small vault, Pit Number Three, was unearthed beside Number Two in June 1976. Only containing one chariot and 69 guards, this is thought to represent the army headquarters. The vault has also been filled in again.

It is planned to open Pits Two and Three to the public in 1989. Work began on constructing a roof in the summer of 1987.

Bronze Chariots In 1981 it was revealed that two bronze chariots had been found 17 metres (56 feet) west of the mausoleum. The oldest chariots ever discovered in China, and in remarkably good condition, they show the Qin period's highest artistic standards. Even today they are considered extraordinary works of art.

Each chariot is drawn by four horses, 72 centimetres (2 feet 4 inches) high by one metre (3 feet 3 inches) in length. Originally painted white, now turned to grey, they bear harnesses inlaid with gold and silver.

Each quadriga has a bronze carriage with an awning of thin sheet bronze, painted with cloud and geometric patterns. The drivers of the original pair are dressed as ninth-grade officials. One stands 91 centimetres (3 feet) high, while the other is sitting. It is believed that the figures were first modelled in clay and then cast in bronze. They may be part of a procession.

Equally astounding treasures probably lie north, south and west of the mausoleum; but Chinese archaeologists have remained tight-lipped in the face of such speculations, and it is unlikely that any further discoveries will be published until thorough examinations have taken place.

Qin Ling, the Mausoleum of the First Emperor

Qin Shihuangdi began supervising the construction of Qin Ling, the tomb where he is buried, as soon as he took the throne in 246 BC. Work intensified after the conquest of the rival states, with 700,000 labourers conscripted to build it. The site chosen was south of the Wei River beside the slopes of Black Horse Mountain in what is now Lintong Country, 30 kilometres (18 miles) from Xi'an.

The outside of the mausoleum is in the form of a low earth pyramid with a wide base. Preliminary investigation by the Chinese has confirmed that there were an inner and an outer enclosure. The mausoleum is suspected to have been plundered at least once, by a rebel general called Xiang Yu (Hsiang Yu) in 206 BC. But no excavations have yet been done. Chinese archaeologists are reluctant to open up the tomb until they know a way to preserve what may be very delicate remains.

It is known, however, that not only was the body of Qin Shihuangdi interred in the tomb (in 209 BC, a year after his death), but also those of his childless wives — who were buried alive — together with artisans who had knowledge of the inner structure of the mausoleum.

Information about the construction of the mausoleum comes almost entirely from the brush of Sima Qian (Ssu-ma Ch'ien), the author of *The Historical Records*, China's first large-scale work of history which was written about a century after the fall of Qin.

According to Sima, heaven and earth were represented in the central chamber of the tomb. The ceiling formed the sky with pearls for stars. The floor was a physical map of the world in stone; the 100 rivers of the empire flowed mechanically with mercury. All manner of treasures were piled inside for the emperor's opulent after-life. Crossbows were set up and positioned to shoot automatically if the interior was disturbed. After it was sealed the tomb was grassed over to appear as a natural hill. It is still like that today, although a stairway has now been built to the top, from which there is a good view of the surrounding area.

Near the mausoleum many ancillary tombs have been discovered. Some occupants were probably victims of the Second Emperor in the power struggle following the death of Qin Shihuangdi. In addition, some large graves, suspected to be those of Qin Shihuangdi's parents, have also been discovered in the area, as well as the graves of a general and of some 70 Qin labourers together with large numbers of horse skeletons. None of the sites of these finds has so far been put on view to the public.

Remains of Xianyang

The Qin capital Xianyang was built in 350 BC on the north bank of the Wei River. It is said to have developed into a metropolis with 800,000 inhabitants before rebel general Xiang Yu set fire to it in 206 BC.

In 1961 the exact location of the city was re-discovered in the Yaodian People's Commune about 15 kilometres (10 miles) northwest of Xi'an. Excavations in the 1960s and 1970s revealed the foundations of the Xianyang Palace, the First Emperor's principal domicile, partly built on a terrace of pounded earth. The structure and the function of different part of the palace are now known. Important discoveries were made including the remains of some murals. Building materials, decorated bricks and tiles were found in large quantities. These remains, and a model of the palace, can be seen in the Xianyang Museum.

Remains of Afang Palace

In 212 BC the First Emperor decided to build a new and larger principal palace on the other side of the Wei River, some 10 kilometres (6 miles) west of Xi'an. Afang Palace was never finished, but the raised platform of pounded earth has remained to this day.

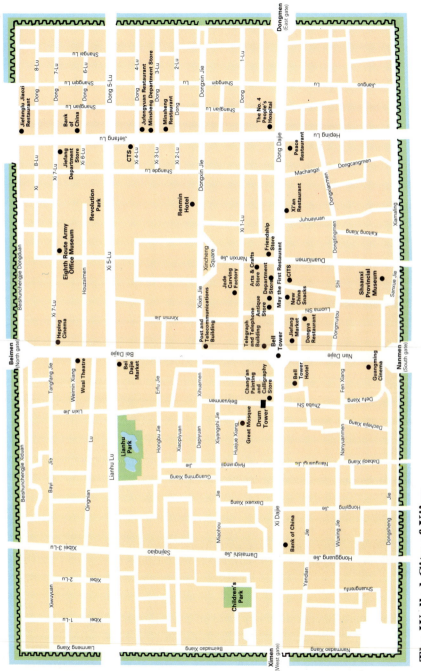

The Walled City of Xi'an

Beimen (North gate)

Ximen (West gate)

Nannmen (South gate)

Dongmen (East gate)

Jiefanglu Jiaozi Restaurant

Bank of China

Jiefang Department Store

Jiefengyuan Restaurant
Minsheng Department Store
Minsheng Restaurant

The No. 4 People's Hospital

CTS

Peace Restaurant

Revolution Park

Rennin Hotel

Xi'an Restaurant

Eighth Route Army Office Museum

Xincheng Square

Friendship Store

Jade Carving Factory

Arts & Crafts Store

Shaanxi Provincial Museum

Heping Cinema

Post and Telecommunications Building

Department Store

May the First Restaurant

CITS

New China Snacks

Telegraph and Telephone Building

Antique Store

Jiefang Market

Bei Dajie Market

Bell Tower

Dongya Restaurant

Wusi Theatre

Chang'an Painting and Calligraphy Store

Bell Tower Hotel

Guangming Cinema

Great Mosque

Drum Tower

Lianhu Park

Children's Park

Bank of China

Period Three: The Han Dynasty

Background

The Qin Dynasty maintained its authority only until 209 BC. The First Emperor's death in 210 BC was followed by outbreaks of rebellion and civil war, which led to the empire's dissolution. The final blow was dealt by General Xiang Yu, who conquered the Qin forces in 207 BC. But then he himself was overthrown four years later by the founder of the Han Dynasty.

The first Han emperor was a general of plebeian background called Liu Bang (Liu Pang), known posthumously by his dynastic title of Han Gaozu (Han Kao-tsu), which literally means Great-great-grandfather of Han. His capital, called Chang'an, was built in the strategic Wei valley. Accordingly the first half of Han rule, lasting until AD 8, is called the Western Han to distinguish it from the Eastern Han period, 25–220, when the capital was at Luoyang.

The Capital City of Chang'an

In 202 BC Liu Bang moved into a minor Qin palace on the southern side of the Wei. Later the architect Xiao He added a large new complex of some 40 buildings to the west of it. This was the Weiyang Palace (see page 65), which was to remain the principal seat of the Western Han emperors. Together these two palaces formed the nucleus of Han-Dynasty Chang'an.

The imperial establishment soon outgrew the two original palaces and more buildings were added during the time of the Emperor Han Huidi (reigned 194–187 BC). An irregular-shaped wall was built around the palaces, eventually forming a circumference of about 22 kilometres (14 miles). Within the wall there were eight main streets and 160 alleys. Outside the wall another city developed, a city of artisans, with markets, workshops and houses.

The Silk Road

It was during the Han that central and western Asia was opened up to the Chinese. This was to have a profound impact on Chang'an.

From the capital, Han Wudi, the Martial Emperor (reigned 140–86 BC), launched a series of campaigns against the Xiongnu, the warlike Turkish people of the steppes, who were a constant threat to the northern frontier of China. In 139 BC Zhang Qian (Chang Ch'ien) was sent officially to central Asia to find allies against the Xiongnu. On his second journey in 119 BC he went as far as the Ili Valley, on the present-day border with the Soviet Union, and from there despatched envoys to India and the Iranian Empire as well as kingdoms east of the

Caspian Sea. One of the most influential finds that Zhang Qian made on this journey were the splendid horses in what is now Soviet Uzbekistan. Some of these were brought to China where they later became the inspiration of Chinese sculptors, painters and writers to an extent that was almost obsessional, especially during the Tang Dynasty.

Merchant caravans followed the armies and established the routes of what Europeans later called the Silk Road. The eastern section opened by the Chinese linked up with trade routes in western Asia to form lines of trade and cultural exchange stretching from Chang'an to the Mediterranean. Official contact with the Roman Empire was attempted in AD 97, but the envoy never got through. However, unofficial representatives of Rome, including a party of jugglers in 120, did arrive in Chang'an. There was a special street where foreigners were accommodated, and even a protocol department to arrange the formal side of their reception.

Paper was one of many Chinese inventions that eventually reached Europe via the Silk Road. The world's earliest pieces of paper were discovered in 1957 at Ba Bridge, east of Xi'an. It was originally thought that paper was invented during the Eastern Han, but these pieces of hemp paper were made considerably earlier, during the reign of Han Wudi.

The Imperial Tombs of the Western Han Dynasty
There are nine tombs of the Western Han emperors on the north bank of the Wei and two south of the present city of Xi'an. The construction of each one was started soon after the accession of the sovereign and, according to regulations, one-third of all State revenues was devoted to the project. On the death of the emperor valuable objects were placed in the tomb and the body was interred in a suit of jade plates, sewn together with gold wire. A piece of jade was placed in the mouth of the emperor. Prominent members of the imperial family and important officials were buried in smaller ancillary or satellite tombs nearby.

None of the imperial mausoleums has been excavated, and they remain irregular flat-topped grassy pyramids, 33−46 metres (110−50 feet) above the plain.

Sights

Mao Ling, the Mausoleum of Emperor Han Wudi
Mao Ling is the tomb of Han Wudi (Han Wu-ti), the Martial Emperor, who came to the throne in 140 BC, ruling for 54 years. Like Qin Shihuangdi, he initiated a new period of dynamic expansion.

Imperial rule was extended to the southeastern coastal region of China, northern Vietnam and northern Korea. His tomb is 40 kilometres (25 miles) west of Xi'an. Although it has not been excavated, the commemorative area has been well laid out. The top of the small hill on which a monument has been built commands a good view of many surrounding tombs, only some of which have been excavated.

The Martial Emperor had tried to avoid his burial with attempts at making himself immortal. He put a bronze statue (the Brazen Immortal) in a high tower to catch the pure dew in a bowl, which he drank with powdered jade. However, the potion proved ineffective, and he died in his 70th year. Apparently there were so many treasures intended for his tomb that they could not all be fitted in. But many of his books are said to have been buried with him, as well as a number of live animals.

The mausoleum was desecrated, rather than robbed, by peasant rebels called the Red Eyebrows just before the establishment of the Eastern Han. They removed articles from the tomb and threw them on a bonfire. Archaeologists believe that they have found the patch of burnt earth where this happened.

Mao Ling is situated northwest of Xi'an, a convenient stop on the way to or from Qian Ling, the Tang-Dynasty tombs (see page 78).

The Tomb of Huo Qubing

About one and a half kilometres (under a mile) from the mausoleum of the Martial Emperor is the even more interesting tomb of his eminent general, nicknamed the 'Swift Cavalry General'. Huo Qubing, later Grand Marshal, was born in 140 BC. His uncle took him to fight the fierce northern nomads, the Xiongnu, when he was 18. He died at the age of only 24. According to the author Sima Qian, who was a contemporary, the Martial Emperor built a special tomb for him in the shape of the Qilian Mountain (which marks the present-day border of Gansu and Qinghai Provinces), where Huo had won a great victory.

The tomb has been almost certainly identified by the discovery of 16 remarkable stone sculptures. All are at the site. They are of horses (one of them apparently trampling a Xiongnu), various animals including a tiger, boar, elephant and ox, and two strange human figures, perhaps demons or gods, one of which is wrestling with a bear. This last stone, about 2.77 metres (nine feet) high, may represent a Xiongnu idol. Huo Qubing brought back at least one of these, known as the 'Golden Man'.

On top of the steep-sided tomb mound is a derelict temple. This dates to the last dynasty and has no connection with the tomb.

Museum Beside the two galleries where the stone sculptures are displayed there is a museum. The exhibits are almost all of the Western Han period and were discovered in the area of the Mao Ling.

There are a number of bronze articles, including money, agricultural implements and a magnificent rhinoceros, though the latter is now in the Shaanxi Museum and only a reproduction is on display. There are also examples of the decorated building materials for which both the Qin and Han were famous.

Remains of the Han City of Chang'an

Han City Walls The site of the Han capital is on the northwestern edge of the present-day city of Xi'an. Today, the walls are still there but inside the palaces have been replaced by fields of wheat and rapeseed.

Remains of Weiyang Palace The southern part of the Han city was excavated in 1957–9 so the layout of the palaces is known. The raised area of the audience hall of Weiyang Palace, the principal seat of the Western Han emperors, can be reached by road. The platform is 101 metres (330 feet) long, much smaller than was thought for the original hall, but we know that the Weiyang was rebuilt several times during the Tang period, so it is likely that the foundations have been altered.

Han City Armoury Built in 200 BC, the armoury occupied 23 hectares (57 acres) near the present-day village of Daliuzhai, next to the site of Weiyang Palace. Excavations have revealed a large number of iron weapons, and some made of bronze. At the end of 1981 it was announced that a number of hefty suits of armour had been found weighing 35–40 kilograms (77–88 pounds).

Han-Dynasty gilt horse, unearthed at Mao Ling

Period Four: The Tang Dynasty

Background

The collapse of the Han Dynasty in 220 after years of insoluble economic and political problems was followed by centuries of power struggles, barbarian invasions and political fragmentation, with interludes of unity and order. In 581 a high-ranking official, Yang Qian, seized the throne and founded the Sui Dynasty.

The Sui and the Capital City of Daxingcheng
The old Han city of Chang'an was by then too derelict to serve as the symbol of power of the first Sui emperor, who reigned with the title of Wendi (Wen-ti). He commissioned a brilliant engineer, Yuwen Kai, to build a new city — Daxingcheng, or the City of the Great Revival — southeast of the old one.

Yang Qian and Yuwen Kai created one of the greatest, perhaps *the* greatest of all planned cities. The huge rectangular area designated for the metropolis faced the four cardinal points and had an outer wall with a circumference of over 36 kilometres (22 miles).

The Sui Dynasty was, however, short-lived. Wendi was succeeded by his even more ambitious son, the Emperor Sui Yangdi (Sui Yang-ti). He, in his turn, ordered the construction of a new capital at Luoyang, as well as a huge programme of canal building (the Grand Canal, the world's largest man-made waterway running from Luoyang to Hangzhou, was his most monumental legacy to China). He also attempted a disastrous invasion of Korea. Rebellions followed and the emperor was assassinated in Yangzhou in 618.

The Establishment of the Tang Dynasty
Power was next seized by the Li family. Li Yuan, hereditary Duke of Tang, marched on Daxingcheng in 617 and in the following year made himself emperor with the title of Tang Gaozu (T'ang Kao-tzu). The capital was renamed Chang'an, a deliberate move to assume by implication the mantle of the Han. In turn, Tang Gaozu was ousted by his second son Li Shimin, who took the throne himself with the title of Tang Taizong (T'ang T'ai-tsung), and effectively consolidated the Tang.

The Tang Dynasty is widely considered to be a Golden Age, the point in history when Chinese civilization reached its most glorious and sophisticated stage. The Tang empire was the largest, richest, most advanced state in the world. And Xi'an (Chang'an) was again the centre and symbol of this glory, the world's largest and most splendid city. Only the Baghdad of Harun al Rashid offered any comparison. During the Tang, Xi'an's city wall stretched far beyond the one

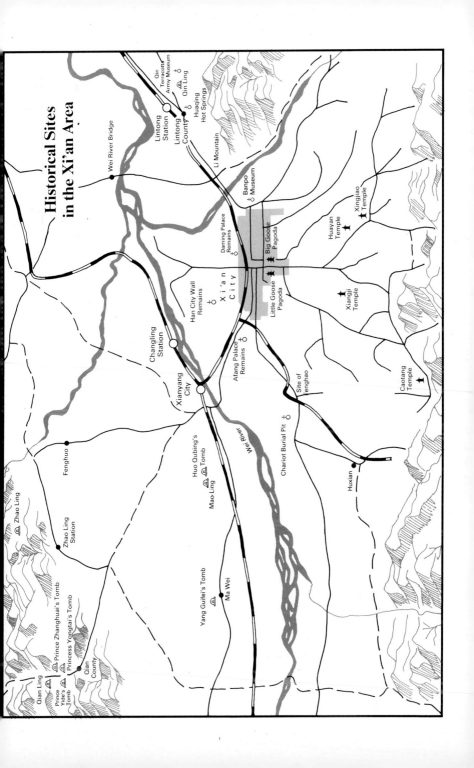

Historical Sites in the Xi'an Area

Qin Terracotta Army Museum

Qin Ling

Lintong Station

Lintong County

Huaqing Hot Springs

Wei River Bridge

Li Mountain

Banpo Museum

Xingjiao Temple

Daming Palace Remains

Big Goose Pagoda

Huayan Temple

Han City Wall Remains

Xi'an City

Little Goose Pagoda

Changling Station

Xiangji Temple

Afang Palace Remains

Xianyang City

Site of Fenghao

Caotang Temple

Chariot Burial Pit

Fenghuo

Huo Qubing's Tomb

Wei River

Huxian

Mao Ling

Zhao Ling

Zhao Ling Station

Yang Guifei's Tomb

Ma Wei

Qian County

Prince Zhanghuai's Tomb

Princess Yongtai's Tomb

Qian Ling

Prince Yide's Tomb

standing today, which was built during the later Ming period, and went as far as the Big Goose Pagoda. By the middle of the eighth century China had a population estimated at 53 million, of which nearly two million lived in the capital.

Empress Wu

Taizong died in 649 and was succeeded by his ninth son, who reigned with the title of Gaozong until 683. However, the next effective ruler was a woman, not a man. Wu Zetian (see page 74) was born in 624 and became a concubine of Taizong. On his death she withdrew from Court and became a Buddhist nun, only to be recalled by Gaozong and eventually become his empress in 655.

After Gaozong's death Wu Zetian dethroned two of her sons and her official reign began in 690. Although Empress Wu's rule was characterized by recurrent palace intrigues and ruthless political murders, China prospered greatly during her reign.

For economic as well as political reasons she preferred Luoyang to Chang'an and the capital was in the former city from 683 to 701. Just before her death in 705, when she was in her 80s, she was finally removed from power, and the Tang re-established.

The Reign of Emperor Tang Xuanzong

The period of struggle over the Tang succession was ended through the emergence of the third great ruler of the dynasty, Emperor Xuanzong, Empress Wu's grandson. Popularly known as Ming Huang, the Enlightened Emperor, his reign corresponds with what is called the High Tang, the apogee of the Tang Dynasty, that most confident and cosmopolitan of all phases of Chinese civilization.

The emperor presided over a brilliant, extravagant Court, patronizing the greatest concentration of literary and artistic genius in Chinese history. Xuanzong's contemporaries included the paramount poets of China, Du Fu (Tu Fu, 712–70) and Li Bai (Li Po, 699–762), and the greatest of painters, Wu Daozi (Wu Tao-tzu, 700–60).

After the death of his beloved Imperial Concubine (see page 80), Xuanzong died a broken man in 762, having earlier abdicated in favour of his third son.

Chang'an in the Eighth Century

Chang'an in the eighth century was a lively, crowded, beautiful city. Appropriately, as the planned capital of a well-ordered society, it was also a highly organized city.

In the centre was the Imperial City with the Imperial Secretariat, the Imperial Chancellery, the Censorate and the Department of State Affairs under which came the Six Boards of Personnel, Revenue,

Rites, War, Justice and Public Works. This organization of government lasted, in form at least, for the next thousand years.

The central north—south avenue, with the delightful name of 'The Street of the Vermilion Bird', divided the Outer City into two districts: the area of the aristocrats to the east, and the rather more populated section of the merchants and lower classes to the west. The two markets which served them were very large and extremely well run. We know that the shops and workshops of the East Market were divided into 220 trades, each one with its own exclusive area, its own bazaar.

Much of the colour in Chang'an was provided by the 'Westerners' — the streets thronged with merchants from central Asia and Arabia, and particularly with travellers from Persia.

Central Asian fashions dominated the capital. Women dressed in the Persian style and wore exotic Western jewellery. Men played polo. The various Buddhist temples and monasteries of the capital vied with each other in offering unusual religious entertainments.

Foreigners congregated in the West Market, which was always full of excitement and activity. Here were bazaars and artisans' workshops, merchants' houses and hostelries, taverns and entertainment places, including wine shops where the songs and dances of central Asia were performed. There were Persian bazaars; shops of the unpopular Uygur (Uighur) moneylenders; and markets selling precious jewels and pearls, spices, medicinal herbs, silk, and a whole range of everyday items, including the newly-fashionable beverage, tea. A place of tremendous variety, the West Market was where criminals were punished and where courtesans could be found. Many of these ladies were from the lands bordering Persia and some were reputedly even blond and blue-eyed.

Foreign Religions in Chang'an
For much of the Tang the authorities allowed the foreign communities freedom of religion. Zoroastrianism, Manichaeism, Nestorianism and finally Islam all followed Buddhism to Chang'an (see section on Buddhism, pages 88—9).

If you are interested in tracing the development of these religions, Xi'an's Shaanxi Museum (see page 106) provides some intriguing evidence. Here you can see a tombstone, dated 874, inscribed in Chinese and Persian Pahlavi script, originally marking the grave of Ma, wife of Suren, a Zoroastrian. Also at the museum, in the Forest of Steles is the celebrated Nestorian Stele. Inscriptions on this stone, in Chinese and Syriac, record the establishment of Chang'an's second Nestorian Christian chapel in 781.

The Manichees, who believed in a combination of Gnostic Chris-

tianity and Zoroastrianism, also had a place of worship in Chang'an in the eighth century.

The Influence of Chang'an

If Chang'an itself was cosmopolitan, it also had unparalleled influence throughout central and eastern Asia. The royal progeny of several Korean and central Asian states, as well as Tibet, were educated in the schools and monasteries of the Tang capital. But by far the greatest transfer of Tang culture was to Japan. From the mid-seventh century to the end of the ninth a whole series of official missions were sent by sea to China. The Japanese cities of Nara and Kyoto were built on the same plan as Chang'an, though naturally smaller. The regular layout of Kyoto still remains today, and the best examples of Tang wooden architecture also survive in Japan rather than in China.

Tang-Dynasty gold coffin and silver outer casket

The Destruction of Chang'an

In the ninth century Chang'an's importance waned, with the Tang Dynasty itself coming under pressure as factions jostled for power. Twice Chang'an was sacked by peasant rebels and troops of the imperial forces. In 904 the Tang Court was moved to Luoyang. The main surviving buildings were dismantled and the beams were taken to the Wei River where they were lashed together to form rafts which were floated down to the new capital. Between 904 and 906 the city walls were demolished and a new, more modest, wall was put up around the old Imperial City. In 907 the last Tang emperor was finally deposed and Chang'an was renamed Daanfu.

The Imperial Tombs of the Tang Dynasty

From the tomb of the Emperor Xuanzong in the east to the tomb of

Empress Wu

The Golden Age of the Tang Dynasty was ushered in not by an emperor but by an ex-concubine, who became the only woman sovereign in Chinese history. Wu Zhou's remarkable career began in 638 when she entered the palace, aged 13, as a junior concubine to Emperor Taizong. On his death 11 years later she was relegated to a Buddhist nunnery, as custom dictated, but by then — so it is traditionally alleged — she had already become the mistress of his son, Gaozong. She returned to Court as Gaozong's favourite concubine, set about arranging the murder of the empress and other female rivals, and within a few years gained the rank of imperial consort for herself. Her ascendancy was not achieved without ruthless dispatch of many opponents — ministers who had enjoyed the emperor's trust, members of the imperial family, and all those courtiers who claimed that her relationship with Gaozong was incestuous.

For much of Gaozong's long reign (649–83) real power was in the hands of Empress Wu. She fully exploited his weakness and her own skill for intrigue. Purges of rivals — who were murdered or exiled — kept her position secure, but historians agree that it could not have been sustained had she not possessed great intelligence and a genius for administration. Although she was whimsical, superstitious and highly susceptible to the flattery of any sorceror and monk who could win her favour, she remained for most of her rule consistently adept at picking competent statesmen and military leaders to carry out her policies. The conquest of Korea and defeat of the Turks were accomplished during her time. The imperial examination system — by which government officials were chosen regardless of their social standing — was promoted, so that in time political power was transferred from the aristocracy to a scholar-bureaucracy. She was, as one historian put it, 'not sparing in the

Gaozong and Empress Wu in the west, the 18 Tang tombs are spread out in a line 120 kilometres (75 miles) long. Most of them are set into natural hills and mountains, rather than underneath artificial mounds.

Each tomb was originally surrounded by a square wall and had a series of buildings for ceremonial purposes and for the use of the guards. Each had its own 'Spirit Way', an avenue lined with stone sculptures. The Tang conception was much grander than that of the well-known Ming Tombs in Beijing, where all 13 tombs share a common approach.

The underground palaces of the emperors remain untouched. Only the important subsidiary tombs of the Zhao Ling and the Qian Ling have been excavated.

---

bestowal of titles and ranks, because she wished to cage the bold and enterprising spirits of all regions. . . but those who proved unfit for their responsibilities were forthwith, in large numbers, cashiered or executed. Her broad aim was to select men of real talent and true virtue.' During her years in power the stability of the empire laid the foundation for the prosperity and cultural achievements that followed and culminated in the High Tang.

Empress Wu bore Gaozong four sons and one daughter. Their second son was named heir-apparent in 675 but Empress Wu, suspecting him of an attempted coup, banished the prince to Sichuan. It was there that he was subsequently made to take his own life, on his mother's orders. When the emperor died, another of Empress Wu's sons was enthroned. He proved to be as ineffectual as his father, and was speedily deposed and exiled as well. The reign of the next crown prince was equally short. In 690, Empress Wu dispensed with puppet emperors altogether by proclaiming a new dynasty — Zhou — and usurping the throne. Her title, Wu Zetian (Wu is Heaven), underscored her claim to the Mandate of Heaven.

While Wu Zetian continued to govern effectively, the last decade of her reign was overshadowed by several more savage murders. By now in her 70s, the old empress was becoming increasingly dependent on two corrupt courtiers, the Zhang brothers. Their malevolent presence was intensely loathed by the rest of the Court, and it was their insinuations that impelled Wu Zetian to order the execution of her granddaughter, her step-grandson and another Wu relative on a charge of disloyalty. The Zhang brothers were finally killed in a palace coup in 705, which forced the empress to abdicate in favour of her exiled son and restore the Tang. She died less than a year later.

Sights

Huaqing Hot Springs

A must for every visitor to Xi'an, the Huaqing Hot Springs have been a favourite spa site of the Tang Dynasty. For centuries emperors had come here to bathe and enjoy the scenic beauty. It remains an ideal spot for relaxation. The more energetic visitors may climb some or all of Li Mountain, on which are situated several Daoist (Taoist) and Buddhist temples. None of the buildings in the grounds are particularly important. Although many of them are named after Tang halls and pavilions, they were built either at the end of the last century or during this one.

Huaqing Hot Springs can be conveniently visited on the return from the Terracotta warriors site. A principal pleasure spot for Chinese tourists, the place is nearly always packed, and especially so on Sundays.

The resort dates back to the Western Zhou when a series of pleasure resort palaces began to be built at the hot springs site, which is 30 kilometres (18 miles) from Xi'an, at the foot of Black Horse Mountain. The First Emperor of Qin had a residence there, as did Han Wudi, the Martial Emperor. In more recent times even Chiang Kai-

shek used some of the buildings. However, the strongest associations are with the Tang: Black Horse Mountain is still covered with the pine and cypress planted by Tang Xuanzong, and the present buildings have a Tang atmosphere.

Taizong commissioned his architect Yan Lide (Yen Li-te) to design a palace, the Tangquan, in 644. It became the favourite resort of Xuanzong, who spent every winter there from 745 to 755 in the company of Yang Guifei, the Imperial Concubine. The resort was much enlarged in 747 and renamed Huaqing Palace. The complex was destroyed at the end of the Tang.

The Baths The best way to appreciate the Huaqing Hot Springs is, of course, to take a bath. The water rises at a constant temperature of 43°C (109°F) and contains various minerals, including lime and manganese carbonate. Over 400 people can be accommodated at the springs at one time. The Emperor's Nine Dragon Bath can be hired by four people for Rmb10 for 40 minutes. The Lotus and Crabapple Baths both take a couple for Rmb5 for 40 minutes, and there are other cheaper baths. Best of all, perhaps, are the baths of the Huaqing Guesthouse (see page 29), which can be hired at Rmb12 an hour for two people. Arrangements for these can be made at the building on the right as you enter the west gate.

The Imperial Concubine's Bath is said to be on the site of the Hibiscus Bath, used by Yang Guifei. The site of the real Tang baths, next to the Imperial Concubine's Bath, is still (1987) being excavated and re-built.

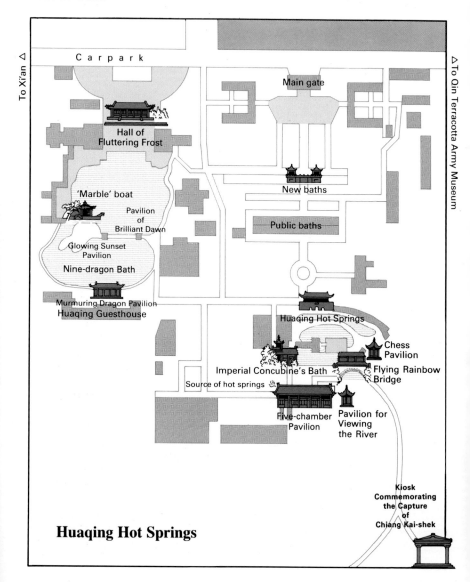

Huaqing Hot Springs

The Site of the Xi'an Incident The Five-chamber Building, just behind the Imperial Concubine's Bath, contains the bedroom used by Chiang Kai-shek on the eve of the Xi'an Incident in 1936 (see page 102), when Chiang fled and hid from his rebellious troops. The position of his hiding place is now marked by an iron chain. The Kiosk Commemorating the Capture of Chiang Kai-shek was originally erected by the Nationalists to celebrate the escape of their leader and named the Pavilion of National Regeneration.

Qian Ling

Of all the imperial tomb complexes near Xi'an the Qian Ling is probably the best preserved and the most complete. It is the mausoleum of Emperor Tang Gaozang and Empress Wu Zetian (see page 74) and is situated 85 kilometres (53 miles) west of Xi'an. It has never been robbed or excavated but there are interesting relics in its vicinity.

If you stand at the southern approach to the mausoleum you can appreciate the original Tang layout and design. This main southern approach is between two prominent small hills, surmounted with towers built in the eighth century. From a distance, the hills greatly resemble a pair of human breasts, incurring the tale that Emperor Tang Gaozang had them constructed to honour the natural beauty of his wife. Beneath them are two obelisk-like Cloud Pillars and then a series of pairs of stone statues lining the route to the mausoleum.

This grand and imposing avenue of animal and human statues leading all the way up to the tombs is perhaps Qianling's most impressive feature, creating a memorable and awe-inspiring effect.

First there are two winged horses, then two vermilion birds like ostriches. Five pairs of saddled horses come next, originally each with a groom. These are followed by ten pairs of tall, almost hieratic figures of guardians. They have very large heads, wear long-sleeved robes, and hold the hilts of long swords that rest on the ground in front of them.

Beyond the guardians are two stone memorials: the one on the left (west) commemorates the reign of Tang Gaozong and is balanced on the east side by the so-called Blank Tablet in honour of Empress Wu. The original implication was apparently that the old empress was beyond praise, but memorials were in fact inscribed on it during the Song and Jin Dynasties (960–1234).

North of the two ruined towers is a remarkable collection of 61 now headless stone figures. From inscriptions on the backs of these figures it appears that they represent actual foreigners who came to the Chinese Court in the seventh century. Some are envoys of central

Asian countries, some are barbarian chiefs. Behind them are two powerful sculptures of stone lions, guarding the southern entrance to the original inner enclosure, now no longer extant. There are similar pairs of animals at the north, east and west entrances. Just inside the old southern entrance is an 18th-century stele.

The Qian Ling Satellite Tombs

To the southeast of the principal mausoleum are 17 satellite tombs beneath man-made mounds. The names of the occupants are all known. Five of the tombs were excavated between 1960 and 1972.

Yang Guifei

Yang Guifei was a concubine whose love affair with Emperor Xuanzong of the Tang Dynasty eventually brought about his downfall and the collapse of Xi'an's Golden Era. Her renowned beauty, and her power, have become legendary in China.

When Emperor Xuanzong had firmly established a strong empire with a cosmopolitan capital in Xi'an and a brilliant Court, he ordered a search throughout the land to find China's greatest beauty. Thousands of young women — one from as far away as Japan — are said to have been brought before him, only to be discarded or relegated to a secondary status in the back rooms of his palace.

One day, at Huaqing Hot Springs, Yang, the 18-year-old daughter of a high official and concubine of one of the emperor's many sons, caught Xuanzong's eye. Amidst protestations from his son, Xuanzong took Yang to be his own concubine, and she grew to wield enormous influence over the emperor, who began neglecting matters of state to spend time with her. He renamed her Yang Guifei — Yang the Imperial Concubine.

Tang-Dynasty paintings indicate that — like other beauties of the time — Yang Guifei was as plump as an Arab harem queen. Taking great pains to please her, the emperor had the palace at Huaqing Hot Springs enlarged, and she spent many languorous hours bathing there to keep her skin fresh. As the eminent Chinese poet Bai Juyi recounted:

When she bathed in the Huaqing baths,
The warm water slipped down
Her glistening jade-like body.
When maids helped her rise
At once she won the emperor's notice...
Behind the warm lotus-flower curtain,
They took their pleasure in the spring nights,
Regretting only that the nights were too short,
Rising only when the sun was high,

They had previously been robbed, but evidently only of gold, silver and precious gems. Archaeologists found·a large number of pieces of pottery. But by far the most exciting discoveries at the sites were the mural paintings in the interiors. These provide valuable information about Tang Court life, and are exquisite examples of the quality of the period's art.

Unfortunately the paintings started to deteriorate soon after the tombs had been opened. All the principal ones have now been taken to the Shaanxi Museum, and replaced with reproductions which are fairly accurate to the originals.

He stopped attending Court sessions...
Constantly she amused and feasted with him,
Accompanying him on spring outings,
Spending every night with him.
Though there were other ladies in his Court,
Three thousand of rare beauty,
His favours to three thousand
Were concentrated in one body.

As Yang Guifei's spell over the emperor grew, so did her demands. Fresh lychees, her favourite fruit, were brought by pony express from Guangzhou every week. Many of her relatives took positions at Court, with her cousin becoming Prime Minister.

Yang Guifei also caught the eye of a Mongolian Turk, An Lushan, who had become a military governor in northeast China. Visiting the Tang Court often, he was rumoured to have become Yang's lover. Although 15 years her elder, he was — in a bizarre ceremony — adopted as her son. An Lushan became impatient for power, and soon attempted a forceful takeover of the capital.

As his troops neared Xi'an, the emperor fled with Yang Guifei to the west. Years of neglect had weakened the imperial army, and its remaining soldiers were determined to remove Yang Guifei, the cause of its decline. When stopping to change horses at Ma Wei, the soldiers mutinied, killing the Prime Minister, and demanding that the 'moth-like eyebrows' of Yang Guifei be surrendered as well.

A more valiant lover might have given his own life first, but Xuanzong stood by helplessly as Yang Guifei was strangled in the courtyard of a small Buddhist temple. Her tomb is still there today.

The An Lushan rebellion dragged on for several years, but was eventually crushed. The emperor, however, never recovered from his loss of Yang Guifei, and died a broken man a few years later. The Tang Dynasty survived nominally, but a steady decline had set in, and its former glory was never to be regained.

The Tomb of Princess Yongtai (Yung-t'ai) This was the first tomb to be excavated and remains the most impressive of all the tombs that can be seen. Princess Yongtai was a granddaughter of Emperor Gaozong and Empress Wu. She died in 701 at the age of 17.

Her death was dramatic. According to the records she was executed by her ruthless grandmother on suspicion of having criticized some Court favourites (see page 74). Five years after her death her remains were exhumed and her tomb built at the Qian Ling complex. The memorial tablet inside the tomb states that she died in childbirth, perhaps because the manner of her death was considered shameful.

When the tomb was excavated, archaeologists came across an unexpected, gruesome discovery: the skeleton of a tomb robber, evidently murdered by his accomplices. The modern Japanese writer Yasushi Inoue has written a short story, *Princess Yung-tai's Necklace*, based on this incident (see Recommended Reading, page 122).

In contrast to all these chilling associations are the charming murals on the tunnel walls leading down to the princess's tomb. They represent Court attendants, almost all of them women, wearing the elegant central Asian fashions of the day. The stone sarcophagus is also beautifully engraved with figures, birds and flowers. But it is now empty. Archaeologists suspect that the princess's actual remains were buried secretly nearby, but they have never been found.

The Tomb of Prince Yide (I-te) The tomb of Princess Yongtai's half-brother, who died at the age of 19, apparently for the same reason and at the same time as his half-sister, is also dated to the same year as hers, 706.

The ceiling of Prince Yide's tomb is decorated with stars, and the walls with Court ladies and eunuchs, palace guards and hunting attendants. There is also a long mural at the entrance with a 196-man procession of guards massed below the high watchtowers of a palace.

The Tomb of the Heir-Apparent Prince Zhanghuai Prince Zhanghuai was one of Empress Wu's sons. He too fell foul of the formidable empress. He was heir-apparent from 675 to 680, but was then disgraced by his mother and forced to commit suicide in 684, at the age of 31. His tomb was built in about 706. The two main paintings in the tomb are of a polo match on one side, and a hunting cavalcade on the other. There are also representations of foreign emissaries with Court officials.

The two other tombs that have been opened are of the Prime Minister Xue Yuanzhao and General Li Jinxing, and are of lesser importance.

Zhao Ling

Zhao Ling is the tomb of Emperor Taizong, who founded the Tang
Dynasty. It is located in the main peak of Mount Jiuzong, approximately 60 kilometres (40 miles) northwest of Xi'an. Although 14 of the
satellite tombs have been excavated, the emperor's mausoleum itself
has not. The whole necropolis covers an area of some 20,000 hectares
(78 square miles). Visitors are normally taken to see the Zhao Ling
Museum, but not the site on Mount Jiuzong itself.

Taizong was a great military commander who loved horses. Six bas-
reliefs of his favourite mounts including that of his most famous horse,
Quanmo, were originally placed at the northern entrance to the tomb.
Considered masterpieces of Tang sculpture, they are unfortunately no
longer *in situ*. The Quanmo stone, together with one other, was taken
to the University Museum of Philadelphia in 1914. The other four
stones are in the Stone Sculpture Gallery of the Shaanxi Museum, with
plaster reproductions of the two in America. The originals were
broken in several places in 1918, apparently in an attempt to facilitate
their transport abroad.

Museum In this museum are displayed all the artifacts removed from
the excavated satellite tombs. There is a splendid selection of Tang
funerary pottery, both glazed and unglazed, including figurines of
Chinese and central Asians, horses and camels. There are some
fragments of wall paintings, a ceremonial crown from a satellite tomb
and a massive pottery roof finial from the Hall of Offerings, the main
building of the original enclosure in front of the emperor's mausoleum.

The museum also features a Forest of Steles (not to be confused
with the famous one at Shaanxi Museum). This is a collection of 42
vertical memorial tablets which originally stood outside the tomb
mounds, and ten flat tablets from the interiors.

Xingqing Park

This is the most pleasant park in Xi'an. Located east of the city wall's
southeast corner, it is quiet and full of trees. On weekdays it is an
excellent place to get away from the crowds.

The park was originally the site of a Tang palace, where the sons of
Emperor Tang Ruizong (reigned 684−90, 710−12) lived at the beginning of the eighth century. It became known as the Xingqing Palace in
714 after Emperor Xuanzong succeeded his father.

Famous for its peonies, Xingqing was a favourite palace of the
emperor and Imperial Concubine Yang. After the Tang, the land on
which the palace had been built eventually reverted to agricultural use.

The transformation of the site into a park came about in 1958

during the Great Leap Forward. Thousands of citizens were involved
in laying out the park, taking only 120 days to complete the 50-hectare
(122-acre) project.

It has an ornamental lake and a number of Tang-style buildings
bearing the names of famous halls and pavilions in the palace of
Xuanzong. There is also a white marble memorial, erected in 1979, to
Abe no Nakamaro (701–70), a famous secular Japanese visitor to
Chang'an during the Tang, who rose to become a Collator of Texts in
the Imperial Library.

Remains of Daming Palace

Daming Palace, or the Palace of Great Luminosity, was begun by
Taizong in 634 for the use of his father, although Gaozu died before it
was completed. In 663 it was much enlarged for Emperor Gaozong and
from then on became the principal palace of the Tang emperors.

The site of Daming Palace is to the northeast of the walled city, on
the fringe of the modern urban area. It is now largely fields. The
terraces on which once stood Hanyuan Hall (where important
ceremonies were held) and Linde Hall (another large, but informal
complex) may still be seen, together with a depression which was the
ornamental Penglai Pool in Tang times. The whole area was excavated
between 1957 and 1959, and the foundations of some 20 buildings were
discovered. The Linde Hall in particular was completely excavated,
although the site has now been filled in again.

Buddhism during and after the Tang

Background

During the Tang, Chang'an became the main centre of Buddhist learning in east Asia. The first contacts between adherents of Buddhism and the Chinese were probably made with the opening of the Silk Road during the reign of the Martial Emperor, Han Wudi (reigned 140−86 BC). During the following centuries this central Asian route, with Chang'an as its eastern terminus, remained the principal one by which Buddhism reached China.

Today a number of monuments bear witness to the importance of Buddhism in the city's history. Most famous are two prominent landmarks with unforgettable names: the Big and the Little Goose Pagodas (see pages 89 and 93). Also in reasonable condition is Da Cien Temple (of which the Big Goose Pagoda is a part), and two interesting temples south of the city, the Xingjiao and the Xiangji Temples (see pages 95 and 96). Some other Buddhist temples have survived in various states of disrepair but may prove worth visiting, as much for the setting and the journey there as for the temple buildings themselves.

Several of the surviving temples and pagodas have particular associations with Buddhist monks, scholars and translators who made the journey from Chang'an to India in search of enlightenment, the Buddhist scriptures and, perhaps, adventure. Some 200 Chinese monks are recorded as travelling from Chang'an to India between the third and the eighth centuries. A number of central Asian and Indian monks also came to Chang'an, but they are less well documented than the Chinese travellers.

Best known of these monks is Xuanzang (Hsuan-tsang) who is today the most popular figure in the whole history of Chinese Buddhism. The Tang monk, as he is often simply called, is the hero of the long 16th-century Chinese novel *Pilgrimage to the West*, sometimes known as *Monkey*, which is very loosely based on Xuanzang's travels. A scholar and translator, Xuanzang's 17-year journey took him to Nalanda (near Patna), then the greatest centre of Buddhist learning in India.

On his return he became abbot of Da Cien Temple (see page 89), where he spent the rest of his life working on translations of Buddhist texts that he had brought from India. His remains were interred under a pagoda which is part of Xingjiao Temple (see page 95).

By the early eighth century, Chang'an had a total of 64 monasteries and 27 nunneries. Much of the scholarship that resulted in the development of two important Buddhist sects — Pure Land and True Word — was done in the city. But the monasteries fulfilled a number of different roles, not only translating, studying and propagating religion, but also patronizing the arts, providing accommodation and even offering some banking facilities. They grew extremely rich, and Buddhism began to enjoy immense popularity at every level of society.

The Tang emperors, however, were ambivalent in their support of the foreign religion. They claimed that Laozi (Lao-tzu), the founder of China's indigenous religion Daoism (Taoism), was their ancestor. Increasingly the success of the great temple-monasteries provoked resistance, and attempts were made to limit their power and wealth. Finally in 841 came a crackdown: the insane Daoist Emperor Tang Wuzong ordered the dissolution of the monasteries and the return of the monks and nuns to secular life. There followed a period of four years of widespread Buddhist persecution when almost all the temple-monasteries were destroyed. Though many of them were refounded after 845, and some of them survive to this day, Buddhism never completely recovered in China. And so, after the destruction of Chang'an at the end of the Tang, the city lost its position as a centre of Buddhist learning for good.

Sights

The Big Goose Pagoda and Da Cien Temple

The Big Goose Pagoda, perhaps the most beautiful building left in Xi'an today, is one of the city's most distinctive and outstanding landmarks. The adjacent Da Cien Temple is the city's best-preserved Buddhist temple complex.

Situated 4 kilometres (2.5 miles) south of the walled city at the end of Yanta Lu, or Goose Pagoda Road, the temple and pagoda are on the site of an earlier Sui temple. Da Cien Temple was established in 647 by Li Zhi (who became Emperor Tang Gaozong in 649) in memory of his mother Empress Wende.

The Big Goose Pagoda The pagoda was completed in 652, and was built at the request of the famous Tang monk, Xuanzang, whose pilgrimage to India is immortalized in the 16th-century Chinese novel *Pilgrimage to the West* or *Monkey*. Xuanzang asked Emperor Gaozong to build a large stone stupa like those he had seen on his travels. The emperor offered a compromise brick structure of five storeys, about 53 metres (175 feet) high, which was completed in 652. This was originally called the Scripture Pagoda. It is said to have served as the place where Xuanzang actually translated into Chinese the Buddhist

scriptures he brought back from India. Its present name, Big Goose
Pagoda, has never been satisfactorily explained.

Between 701 and 704, at the end of the reign of Empress Wu, five
more storeys were added to the pagoda, giving it a sharper, more
pointed form than it has today. It was later damaged, probably by fire,
and reduced to the seven storeys to be seen today. It is a simple,
powerful, harmonious structure, although ironically not how Xuanzang
wanted it to be.

The pagoda rises 64 metres (210 feet) to the north of the other
temple buildings, and is the only remaining Tang building in the
complex. On the pedestal, at the entrance to the first storey, are some
rather faded photographs providing a useful and fascinating survey of
other famous pagodas in China, as well as a number of Tang
inscriptions and engravings set into the base of the pagoda. There are
some delightful tendril designs in bas-relief on the borders of the
tablets and at the top of the tablets some exquisite coiling dragons and
singing angels.

At the southern entrance to the pagoda are copies of prefaces to
the translations of Xuanzang by the emperors Taizong and Gaozong in
the calligraphy of Chu Suiliang (Ch'u Sui-liang). Over the lintel of the
western entrance is an engraving of Sakyamuni and other Buddhist
figures. Other tablets, inscribed during the Ming (1368–1644), recount
the exploits of the Tang monk. On a fine day climb up inside the
internal wooden staircase to the top of the pagoda for a panoramic
view.

Da Cien Temple During the Tang, Da Cien Temple was a considerable
establishment. There were about 300 resident monks and no fewer
than 1,897 rooms around 13 courtyards. It contained paintings by the
leading artists of the day, and had the finest peony garden in the
capital.

Although the temple was one of four to continue functioning after
the great Buddhist persecution of 841–5, it was destroyed at the end
of the Tang (907). Since then it has been ruined and restored several
times, but on a diminished scale. The last major restoration was in
1954, when the pedestal of the pagoda was widened.

The temple entrance is on the south side. Outside is a stone lamp
from the Japanese city of Kyoto. Inside, to the right and left, are the
Bell and Drum Towers, and a path leading to the Great Hall. This
contains three statues of Buddhas, surrounded by 18 clay figures of
Sakyamuni Buddha's disciples. Both the building and the statues inside
are said to date from 1466. To the east of the Great Hall are several
small stone pagodas marking the remains of monks of the Qing period
(1644–1911).

The temple is open from 8.30 am to 6 pm and is accessible by bus number 5 which leaves from the railway station.

The Little Goose Pagoda and Da Jianfu Temple

The Little Goose Pagoda is one of Xi'an's major landmarks. Situated to the south of the walled city, the 13-storey eighth-century pagoda is all that remains of the once flourishing Da Jianfu Temple. The temple, established in 684 in honour of Emperor Gaozong, was particularly associated with the pilgrim Yijing (I-ching), who settled there in the early eighth century to translate texts he had brought back with him from India. Although the temple continued to function after the Buddhist persecutions of 841–5, everything was destroyed save the Little Goose Pagoda, together with an old locust tree said to have been planted during the Tang. Later, more modest temple buildings were erected next to the pagoda.

The pagoda has not survived completely unscathed. When it was completed in 707 the brick structure had 15 storeys, but it was damaged during a series of earthquakes in the late 15th and 16th centuries. In 1487, the pagoda was split from top to bottom by the impact of an earthquake measuring 6.25 on the Richter scale. Amazingly, it did not fall. In 1556 another quake, 8 on the Richter scale, had its epicentre some 75 kilometres (47 miles) east of Xi'an. This one had the effect of throwing the two sides of the pagoda together again, but also dislodging the top two storeys.

The Little Goose Pagoda has remained to this day with only 13 storeys, 43 metres (141 feet) high. There have been conflicting opinions about the original appearance of the building (models of different designs are on display at the temple), which is partly why a complete restoration has never been attempted. Meanwhile, however, the slightly crumbling, open part of its apex gives it a distinct style. A new internal staircase was put up in 1965 so you can climb right to the top and look out over the fields to the walled city to the north. Unlike the Big Goose Pagoda, where the view is confined to narrow windows, you can climb out to an open roof for this panoramic view.

Among the features worth looking out for at the pagoda are some Tang-period engravings of bodhisattvas on the stone lintels at the base of the pagoda. There is also a tablet commemorating a restoration of the pagoda in 1116 and another engraved during the Qing (1644–1911) with information about the earthquakes. A stone tablet dated 1692 gives an interesting idea of what the temple and pagoda would have looked like at that date, except that the pagoda is represented with 15 storeys. Standing in one of the courtyards is a large bell, dated 1192, originally from Wugong County, west of Xi'an, and moved to the

temple about five centuries later. Be sure not to miss the exhibition room (above the room used for official briefings) which has Buddhist statues from the Tang and later dynasties, Buddhist scriptures including some genuine Song and Ming editions, and a series of drawings and photographs of the Little Goose Pagoda.

The pagoda is open from 8.30 am to 5.30 pm.

Xingjiao Temple

This interesting temple is in a very pleasant setting, overlooking the Fanchuan River, 22 kilometres (14 miles) southeast of Xi'an, just beyond the village of Duqu. Xingjiao Temple, or the Temple of Flourishing Teaching, was one of the Eight Great Temples of Fanchuan. It was built in 669 by Tang Gaozong as a memorial to the Tang monk Xuanzang (see page 88), together with a tall brick pagoda covering his ashes. The temple was restored in 828, though by 839 it again lay abandoned according to an inscription on Xuanzang's pagoda. However, it managed to survive until the 19th century when all the buildings were destroyed except the main pagoda and two smaller ones belonging to two of Xuanzang's disciples. The temple was again rebuilt, partly in 1922, partly in 1939. Today, over 30 monks live and worship there.

The three pagodas are in a walled enclosure called the Cien Pagoda Courtyard. The tall central pagoda is dedicated to Xuanzang. It is a beautiful five-storey brick structure, imitating one of wood and with brackets in relief. It probably dates from the ninth century. A small pavilion next to the pagoda has a modern copy of a stone engraving of Xuanzang, carrying the scriptures in what might be described as a sutra-backpack.

On either side of the principal pagoda are those of Xuanzang's two translation assistants. Each is of three storeys. On the west side is that of Kuiji (K'uei-chi, 632–82), nephew of General Yuchi Jingde (a general of Emperor Tang Taizong). It was erected during the Tang. On the other side is the pagoda of Yuance (Yuan-ts'e), a Korean follower of Xuanzang. This was built later, in 1115.

At the entrance to the complex are the Bell and Drum Towers, 20th century but retaining their original instruments of the 19th century or earlier. Facing the entrance is the Great Hall of the Buddha, built in 1939, which contains a bronze, Ming-period Buddha. The Preaching Hall behind was built in 1922 and contains a number of statues including a bronze, Ming-period Amitabha Buddha, and a Sakyamuni Buddha of the same date as the hall.

In the eastern courtyard is the two-storey Library, built in 1922 and restored in 1939. It contains a white jade Buddha from Burma. The library proper is on the upper floor and possesses some Tang-Dynasty sutras, written in Sanskrit, as well as 20th-century editions of the great Tang translations of Xuanzang and others.

You can reach the temple by bus number 5 that leaves from Xi'an's South Gate. The trip takes about 40 minutes.

Daxingshan Temple

Daxingshan Temple was the greatest Buddhist establishment of the Sui and Tang, but since the tenth century it has been destroyed and rebuilt several times. The latest reconstruction was in 1956. Today its grounds have been turned into a small, quiet and charming park (Xinfeng Park). The main buildings have been repainted, and a handful of monks live and worship there.

The temple is said to date back to the third century when it was known as the Zunshan Temple. It was refounded during the Sui when it was given its present name, and became the headquarters of an order with a network of 45 prefectural temples, all established by the founder of the Sui Dynasty, Yang Qian. During the Tang it became a great centre of Buddhist art and learning, and the Tang monk, Xuanzang, hero of the famous Chinese novel *Monkey*, stayed there during the seventh century. Most of the buildings were destroyed during the Buddhist persecution of 841−5, and whatever survived disappeared at the end of the Tang. The temple was rebuilt under the Ming and again restored in 1785 by an expert on Tang-Dynasty Chang'an called Bi Yuan (1730−97). After its reconstruction in 1956 it was used by a community of lamaist monks until the Cultural Revolution (1966−76). Today it houses the Xi'an Buddhist Association.

The temple, in Xinfeng Park, is located south of the Little Goose Pagoda on a small street called Xingshan Si Jie, behind the open market of Xiaozhai.

Xiangji Temple

Xiangji Temple, which has an 11-storey pagoda built in 706, lies due south of Xi'an, some 20 kilometres (12 miles) away, close to the town of Wangqu. The square brick pagoda was built over the ashes of the Buddhist monk Shandao, one of the patriarchs of Pure Land Buddhism which preached salvation through faith rather than meditation. It was built by a disciple named Jingye, who is himself commemorated by a smaller five-storey brick pagoda nearby. Around the pagodas were originally the buildings of one of the great temple-monasteries of Tang Chang'an, although these have long since disappeared.

The pagoda of Shandao is similar in some respects to that of Xuanzang at the Temple of Flourishing Teaching. It has brackets in relief and imitates a wooden structure. If you want to climb the pagoda, try persuading one of the monks for permission. There are about 25 monks who now and live and worship at the temple.

On 14 May l980, which was, by Chinese reckoning, the 1,300th anniversary of Shandao's death in 681, a major restoration of the temple was completed. The Great Hall of the Buddha was rebuilt, and a Japanese Buddhist delegation presented a figure of the monk Shandao. It is now on view inside the hall together with a figure of Amitabha Buddha which was brought from a Beijing museum.

It is difficult to reach the temple by public transport and the journey may take over two hours. Bus number 15 leaves you at a village 6.4 kilometres (4 miles) from the temple, and from there you have to take a second bus which runs irregularly, or walk. But the beautiful surrounding countryside, and, of course the pagodas themselves make the trip well worthwhile.

Song-Dynasty
celadon pot

Caotang Temple

Sometimes translated as the Straw Hut Temple, Caotang Temple was founded during the Tang. Surrounded by fields, it lies about 55 kilometres (35 miles) southwest of Xi'an.

The temple was built on the site of a palace where Kumarajiva, a fourth-century translator of Buddhist scriptures, once worked and taught. Kumarajiva's translations, known for their elegant style rather than for their accuracy, have been used continuously down to modern times. The ashes of Kumarajiva are beneath a stone stupa, thought to be Tang, about two metres (6.5 feet) high, inside a small pavilion. In front there are some old cypress trees and a well. Other temple buildings include bell and tablet pavilions and a main hall.

Located on the road to Huxian, the temple is accessible by taxi or long-distance bus.

Huayan Temple

Huayan Temple was founded by the first patriarch of the Huayan sect of Buddhism, the monk Dushun (Tu-shun, 557−640), during the reign of Tang Taizong. In its heyday, the Huayan Temple, situated in the Fanchuan area 20 kilometres (12 miles) south of Xi'an, was one of the original Eight Great Temples of Fanchuan which flourished during the Tang.

Today, the only part of the temple to have survived are two brick pagodas on the side of a hill. One of them is 23 metres (75 feet) high, and is square, like the Big Goose Pagoda, with seven storeys; the other is smaller with four storeys, and is hexagonal in form. There is a good view of the surrounding area from the pagodas.

Located on the road that passes through Chang'an, southeast of Xi'an, the pagodas are accessible by bus number 15 that leaves from the South Gate (a trip of about 45 minutes) and can conveniently be visited on the way to Xingjiao Temple.

The Temple of the Recumbent Dragon

The Temple of the Recumbent Dragon (Wolongsi), believed to be of Sui foundation, suffered particularly badly during the Cultural Revolution (1966−76). Virtually all the artwork is gone, and only a few portions of one hall remain. It now houses a factory and may be difficult to visit. It is down a dirt path between buildings numbers 25 and 27 along Baishulin Jie, within walking distance of the Shaanxi Museum.

Period Five: Medieval and Modern Xi'an

Background

With the destruction of Chang'an at the end of the Tang, the city lost its political splendour and power for good. Thereafter it remained a regional centre, usually out of the mainstream of political developments. The real economic centre of China had already moved away from Chang'an, further to the southeast, during the late Tang. After 907 the Xi'an area became progressively more impoverished and culturally backward. Much of the history in the following millennium is a dismal repetitious account of droughts and floods, famines and peasant insurrections.

However, Daoism continued to find adherents, and remnants of Daoist temples (see page 111) can be seen in Xi'an today, despite the destruction caused during the Cultural Revolution. Islam, which had first been introduced into Chang'an by Arab merchants during the Tang, also flourished. Xi'an's beautiful Great Mosque is still functioning and welcomes forign visitors (see page 113).

Between the fall of the Tang and the establishment of the Ming Dynasty in 1369, the city changed its name many times. But in 1368 the city was renamed Xi'an Fu, the Prefecture of Western Peace. It was to remain as Xi'an from then on, except for the last year of the Ming Dynasty (1644), when the peasant leader Li Zicheng captured the city and renamed it Chang'an. (The name Chang'an survives today as the name of the county town immediately south of Xi'an.)

The Ming Dynasty

In 1370 Zhu Yuanzhang, the first emperor of the Ming Dynasty, put his second son, Zhu Shuang, in control of Xi'an. Zhu Shuang became Prince of Qin, using the old name for the area. A palace was constructed for him and the city substantially rebuilt on the site of the Imperial City section of the Tang capital, covering approximately one-sixth of the area of the former city. The prince did not take up residence until 1378, when the palace and the walls and gates of the city had already been completed. The palace, which was in the northeast part of the city, no longer exists but much of 14th-century Xi'an still survives, notably the Bell and Drum Towers and the city wall and gates (see pages 110 and 111).

The Qing Dynasty

When the Manchus established the last imperial dynasty of China, the Qing, in 1644, Xi'an was garrisoned by Manchu troops. They occupied the northeast section of the city, which was walled off. In European accounts, these soldiers were referred to, inaccurately, as 'Tartars'.

During the 18th century the city, or at least its officials and merchants, enjoyed some prosperity, as indicated by the great development of Qinqiang opera during this time (see page 43). However, the 19th century was less happy with natural calamities following fast behind a disastrous Muslim rebellion (1862–73).

In 1900 Xi'an again became a capital of sorts during the Boxer War when the Empress Dowager Cixi (Tz'u-hsi, 1835–1908), with her captive nephew, the powerless Emperor Guangxu (Kuang-hsu), fled in disguise from Beijing. They stayed for over a year in Xi'an, beyond the reach of the Western powers, while peace was being negotiated.

In 1911 when a nationwide revolution overthrew the Qing regime, resistance by the garrison in Xi'an collapsed without much of a struggle. But a terrible massacre of the Manchus ensued. Between 10,000 and 20,000 died, including a few unlucky foreigners. Most of the buildings in the Manchu quarter were burnt down. Such blood-letting and destruction did not occur in other cities. Much of the killing in Xi'an was evidently done by the Muslims, in revenge for the suppression of their rebellion 40 years earlier.

Xi'an in the Republican Era
During the Republican period of 1911 to 1949 Xi'an gradually became less isolated from the outer world. Before the revolution the city had already established its first telegraph office (in 1885) and international post office (in 1902). The railway did not reach Xi'an until 1934, but Westerners started to visit the city in increasing numbers from the turn of the century onwards, usually making contact with the China Inland Mission, the Scandinavian Alliance Mission or the English Baptists, all of whom were represented in the city. They returned, often to write books, informing (and more often, misinforming) the outside world about 'ancient Sian-fu':

> It will be long before the City of Western Peace becomes the resort of sightseers. Yet Sian and its neighbourhood provide more sights to see than most inland Chinese capitals, in case the blessed day of trains *deluxe* and steam-heated hotels should ever dawn for it. The rolling plain, all round as far as you can see, is full of mounds and barrows; and two noble pagodas invite inspection. Or you can mount the wall and study the whole flat extent of the city; you can ascend the Drum Tower, and from the vast darkness of its loft look out towards the turquoise roofs of the Mahometan mosque, and, beyond these, to the orange gables of the Imperial Palace, where the Grand Dowager pitched her flying tents in 1900.
> (From *On the Eaves of the World* by Reginald Farrar, 1917)

During the struggle for power in the 1920s and '30s, Xi'an was of some strategic importance and once again in its history played a dramatic role: in 1926, it was occupied by a pro-Nationalist Shaanxi general, Yang Hucheng, and was promptly surrounded by an anti-Nationalist force. So began the six-month Siege of Xi'an. When it was finally lifted, some 50,000 were said to have died. Revolution Park marks the place where they were buried (see page 116).

In the struggle between Communist and Nationalist forces, Xi'an came to the forefront in 1936, when Huaqing Hot Springs was the scene of the so-called Xi'an Incident (see below). Chiang Kai-shek, intent on getting rid of domestic Communist opposition before putting up resistance to the invading Japanese, was arrested by two Nationalist

The Xi'an Incident

Xi'an has always been known to the Chinese as a city rich with history, but it only gained recognition in much of the Western world in 1936 when Generalissimo Chiang Kai-shek was kidnapped there by some of his own generals.

The Xi'an Incident, as it became known, held the leadership of China hanging in the balance for a couple of tension-wracked weeks. An intriguing sequence of events brought on the kidnapping and its solution.

In 1936, while Hitler marched in Europe, the Japanese army was steadily tightening its grip on China. Chiang Kai-shek was not so much in control as simply being at the top of a fragile coalition of Chinese warlords and armies spread over China. The Communists had escaped Chiang's pursuit on the Long March and established themselves securely at Yan'an, in the mountains north of Xi'an.

Chiang knew that a head-on conflict with the Japanese army would, if not demolish him, at least weaken his position, and make him vulnerable to the Communists. He decided to appease the Japanese instead, and sent many of his troops to fight the Communists.

But for Zhang Xueliang, one of Chiang's allied generals, this policy of foot-dragging against the Japanese was unacceptable. A bright and courageous young general, Zhang was head of a Manchurian army, and was incensed at the way his home in northeast China had been over-run by the Japanese since 1931. Zhang saw the situation deteriorating further in 1936, when the Japanese made a dramatic attack into Suiyan, a key area north of Beijing. On 4 December, a Nationalist attack on the Communists failed, resulting in a widespread refusal amongst Chiang's troops to continue fighting. Chiang flew to Xi'an to direct the campaign himself.

Zhang saw this as an ideal moment to make a move. He discreetly made contact with the Communists, and at dawn on 12 December, his troops surrounded the palace at Huaqing Hot Springs, where Chiang was generals, Yang Hucheng and the leader of the displaced Northeastern Army, Zhang Xueliang, and forced to agree to join the Communists against the common enemy, the Japanese. Xi'an then became a vital link between the Communist headquarters in Yan'an and the outside world through the establishment of Eighth Route Army Office (see page 117).

During the Sino-Japanese War, Xi'an was bombed, but never occupied, by the Japanese. After the end of the war, the city was controlled by Nationalist troops until it was taken by Communist forces on 20 May 1949. The People's Republic of China was inaugurated less than five months later.

---

quartered. Hearing gunfire, Chiang escaped barefoot in his nightshirt — leaving his dentures behind — scaled a wall, injuring his back, and scurried up an old path on Black Horse Mountain. Thirty of his men were killed defending him.

Zhang's officers combed the area, and one of them found the Generalissimo later that afternoon, shivering and in pain, crouched in a crevice between the rocks. As the officer moved to bind Chiang's hand, the Generalissimo reminded his captor that he was the Commander-in-Chief. The officer is said to have bowed politely to Chiang and replied, 'You are also our prisoner.'

Two weeks of tough negotiations followed. Chiang and his formidable wife, Soong Mei-ling, were on one side, with Zhang and Zhou Enlai, later Communist China's Premier, on the other, while the rest of China waited impatiently. Many of the Communist leaders wanted to execute Chiang, or at least keep him imprisoned. But a cable arrived from Moscow with an order from Stalin to release Chiang and get on with the task of fighting the Japanese.

The Chinese Communists bristled at being told by 'Uncle Joe' how to handle what they saw as their own affair. But they also knew they could win some useful concessions out of Chiang if they released him.

In the end, a compromise was reached. Chiang was allowed to fly back to Nanjing a free man, but had to give up the pretence of being the sole leader of China. Ostensibly he joined with the Communists in a 'National Front' against the Japanese. Zhang Xueliang, who also went back to Nanjing, was a hero only temporarily and soon arrested by Chiang and branded a traitor.

The visitor to Huaqing Hot Springs can still see the site of this famous incident. The rooms where Chiang lived and worked at the palace are marked, as is the spot up the hill where the Generalissimo was actually caught. The hiding place is marked by a chain and nearby, commemorating the capture, is a kiosk of dignified Grecian structure.

Village life observed — houses dug out of loess embankments can be seen in the Xi'an countryside

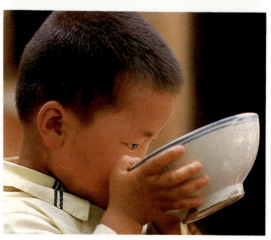

Xi'an under the People's Republic

Xi'an has grown much larger in the past 30 years, both in size and population. Many new industries have also been established. The initial impetus for this growth came from the Government whose policy was to give priority to the development of cities in the interior.

In 1949 Xi'an did not extend much further than the walled city, covering only 13.2 square kilometres (5 square miles). Today the city has spread out to cover some 100 square kilometres (38.5 square miles), an area even larger than the Tang capital of Chang'an which had an area of 81 square kilometres (31.2 square miles), within the outer walls. The modern city is not so regular in its layout as its great pedecessor, and it extends further to the east and west than the Tang city.

The population has increased rapidly since the 1930s when it was between 200,000 and 300,000. Today it is 3.4 million. This includes the people living in seven urban districts, one county (Chang'an) and 70 collectives. The urban population is probably around 2 million.

If you want to see something of the city's recent industrial and social development, CITS can arrange visits to model factories, hospitals, schools, district neighbourhoods, and farming communities, although these are no longer included as a matter of course on tour itineraries.

Another place of major·interest to foreign visitors is the Shaanxi Museum. Although developed earlier, it was formally established in 1952. This is the principal museum of Shaanxi Province and is one of the best of its kind in China.

Sights

Shaanxi Museum

The Shaanxi Museum, one of the finest museums in China, was formally established in 1952 and occupies the former Temple of Confucius. It is the principal museum for Shaanxi Province and displays artifacts brought from every part of the area. It is particularly famous for its Forest of Steles. The 2,600-odd exhibits are shown in chronological order to illustrate the history of Shaanxi — the usual organization of museums in China. Only the large stone sculptures are separate from this arrangement.

The Zhou, Qin and Han Gallery

In front of this first gallery is a fifth-century stone horse from the north of the province. The gallery itself contains items dating from earliest times down to AD 220. There is a good collection of Zhou bronzes, pottery and jade. This includes a massive bronze *ding* tripod. From the Warring States period (475−221 BC) there are various iron agricultural implements as well as rather an amusing item: a fine gold and silver inlaid bronze wine vessel, or *zun*, in the form of a rhinoceros which was found near the tomb of Han Wudi, the Martial Emperor. From the Qin (221−207 BC) there are a number of objects discovered in and around the county town of Lintong, near the mausoleum of the First Emperor of Qin. There are Qin pottery figures, iron weights, coins and decorated building materials. The wide selection of Han-Dynasty pieces include painted clay figurines, pottery models of buildings, weapons and decorated tiles and water pipes. There is a jade seal of an empress of the Western Han (206 BC-AD 8).

The Sui and Tang Gallery

Opposite the stone horse which is outside the first gallery there is an eighth-century Tang bronze bell. This is at the southern entrance of the Sui and Tang Gallery, which covers the period from AD 581 to 907. But if you want to view the exhibits chronologically, you should enter the gallery at the north entrance.

The Tang pottery on display is of the highest quality, much of it excavated in recent years. There are both painted and unpainted, glazed and unglazed examples. Among the polychrome pieces look out for a superb pottery figure of a soldier in armour, discovered at Liquan and dated to 663. Of the tri-colour glazed statues one of the most interesting is a camel with a small orchestra on its carpeted back. There are also powerful figures of horses, and a number of representations of large-nosed, heavily-bearded central Asians.

Fine engraved Tang gold and silver vessels are in the gallery together with bronze mirrors and silver coins from Persia and Japan. Some copies of tomb murals from the Qian Ling complex (see page 78) are on the walls.

The Stone Sculpture Gallery

This gallery, which is beside the Forest of Steles, has a collection of about 70 sculptures and relief carvings of unrivalled quality. However, not all of the stones are originals (in particular the horse from the tomb of 'Swift Cavalry General' Huo Qubing is a reproduction). The most famous exhibits are the six bas-reliefs, four of them originals, from the Zhao Ling, the Mausoleum of Emperor Tang Taizong (see page 84). There are also a number of large animals which once lined the approaches to imperial tombs of the Han and Tang. At the end of the gallery are some Buddhist statues including a very beautiful torso of a bodhisattva, showing strong Indian influence, and an Avalokites-vara on an elaborate lotus throne. Both are Tang period.

The Forest of Steles

This famous collection of over 1,000 inscribed stones began in 1090
when a large Confucian collection of steles cut in 837 — the oldest
existing texts of the Confucian classics — was moved for safekeeping
to the back of the Temple of Confucius. The collection slowly grew
until by the 18th century it had begun to be called by its present name,
the Forest of Steles. It is the largest collection of its kind in China.
This stone library is now a part of the Shaanxi Museum.

The art of making inscriptions on stone began in China at least as
early as the fourth century BC. The earliest examples that have
survived, which are of this date, are the ten Stone Drums of Qin.
Recording a hunting party led by a Duke of Qin, they were discovered
during the Tang Dynasty at Fengxiang, about 145 kilometres (90 miles)
west of Xi'an. The originals are now in Beijing but a reproduction of
one of them is on display in the Zhou, Qin and Han Gallery of the
museum.

From the Han Dynasty onwards flat stones were cut with either text
or pictures in order to preserve the picture or text as well as to make it
possible to reproduce them on paper by taking rubbings. These
rubbings, made into either scrolls or books, have often served as
models for calligraphy practice.

Unfortunately, all explanatory notes for the collection are in
Chinese so unless you have a competent guide-interpreter you may
well leave impressed but mystified by these grey-black slabs of stone.

As a rough guide, the contents of the Forest of Steles can be
divided into four groups: works of literature and philosophy, historical
records, calligraphy and pictorial stones. The pictorial stones, which
may be of most immediate interest, are in Room Four together with
some stones engraved with historical records. The pictorial stones are
almost all relatively late, Ming (1368–1644) or Qing (1644–1911). As
well as landscapes and portraits — notably of Confucius and
Bodhidarma — there are some fascinating stones with allegorical
pictures and some texts written to appear like pictures (it was a Qing
fashion to create pictures composed of Chinese characters). In Room
Three is the calligraphy collection which is of great importance. There
are two reconstructed examples of the calligraphy of Wang Xizhi
(321–79) which have had immense influence on the art of the brush,
together with pieces by many of the great Tang-Dynasty masters.

If you would like to see the famous Nestorian Stele, cut in 781, it is
in Room Two, immediately to the left of the entrance. This records the
history of the Nestorian Christian community at Chang'an from its
founding in the seventh century by a Syrian missionary. Room One
contains the nucleus of the collection, the set of 114 stones engraved in

837 with the definitive text of the Confucian classics. Inscribed on both sides of the stones, the text uses a staggering total of 650,252 characters.

The museum is located on Baishulin Jie near the South Gate and is open from 8.30 am to 6 pm. Tickets are sold up to 5 pm.

The Bell Tower

Each Ming city had a bell tower and a drum tower. The bell was sounded at dawn and the drum at dusk. The two buildings still exist in many Chinese cities, but those at Xi'an are the best known in China.

The Bell Tower was originally built in 1384 at the intersection Xi Dajie and Guangji Jie. This was the centre of the site of the old Tang Imperial City, where the Tang government offices had been located. The tower was removed in 1582 and rebuilt in its present position in the centre of the southern section of the walled city, overlooking the four avenues which lead to the four gates. It was restored in 1739. Now seemingly enmeshed in overhead trolleybus wires, it is nevertheless proudly regarded as the symbol of the city's centre.

The Bell Tower is set on a square brick platform, each side of which is 35.5 metres (116 feet) long, with an arched gateway at ground level. The platform is 8.6 metres (28 feet) high and on top of it is a triple-eaved, two-storey wooden structure, a further 27.4 metres (90 feet) high. There is a fine view in all directions from the parapet on the second floor. The inside is remarkable as an example of the very intricate roof truss system used in Ming and Qing wooden architecture. The original great bell no longer exists, but a small Ming-period bell is kept in a corner of the brick platform.

The Bell Tower is open from 8.30 am to 5.30 pm.

The Drum Tower

The Drum Tower is quite similar to the nearby Bell Tower, except for its rectangular shape. It was first built in 1380, and restored in 1669, 1739 and 1953. The brick base, on which the wooden structure is built, is 52.6 metres (172 feet) long, 38 metres (125 feet) wide, and 7.7 metres (25 feet) high. A road goes straight through it, under a vaulted archway. The triple-roofed, two-storey wooden building is a further 25.3 metres (83 feet) high off its brick platform. The second storey, which is surrounded by a parapet, is now used as an antique shop, for which it provides a very charming setting. The immediate surroundings are more interesting than those of the Bell Tower. Less encumbered by wires, the Drum Tower looks down on the irregular grey-tiled roofs of the Muslim quarter.

The Drum Tower is open from 8.30 am to 5.30 pm and is located two blocks west of the Bell Tower.

The Ming City Wall and Gates

Xi'an's 14th-century city wall still stands, although today it is
intersected by a few modern roads. It is one of the most impressive city
walls in China and certainly one of the best examples from the Ming.

The circumference is 11.9 kilometres (7.4 miles), and it is 12 metres
(40 feet) high, 12−14 metres (40−6 feet) wide at the top and 15−18
metres (49−59 feet) wide at the bottom. It is surrounded by a moat.

The Ming city gates face the four cardinal points, set off-centre in
each of the sides of the rectangular wall. Originally each gate had two
structures: the gate tower, a triple-eaved building 34.6 metres (114
feet) long, and beyond, on the city wall itself, was the massive,
archers' tower, 53.2 metres (175 feet) in length, with 48 openings on
the outer face from which missiles could be fired on a potential enemy.
The towers above the East Gate, to which visitors are usually taken,
are well preserved; but instead of guardrooms and barracks you will
now find inside them souvenir shops and showrooms.

Renovation work on the wall, initiated in recent years, has been
completed, and it is possible to walk along the top of it. Some of the
carefully reconstructed watchtowers on the ramparts have been
converted to teahouses. There are stairways up by the East, South and
West Gates. New gardens have been created between the wall and
moat, making a pleasant setting for a quiet stroll. Restoration work an
all four gates is near completion.

The Great Mosque

This beautiful mosque lies close by the Drum Tower in Huajue Xiang.
It is surrounded by the old houses and narrow lanes of Xi'an's Muslim,
or *Hui*, community. The mosque is still active: on ordinary days about
500 men pray there, with perhaps 2,000 on Fridays. Of the ten or so
functioning mosques in the city this is the only one which is open to
visitors although non-Muslims are not admitted at prayer times.

Islam has been the most enduring of all faiths in Xi'an. It was first
introduced by Arab merchants during the Tang Dynasty, and flourished during the Yuan (1279−1368). The Muslims gradually became
concentrated in the northwestern part of the walled city, where they
remain to this day. The community now numbers about 30,000. There
were said to be 14 mosques open before the Cultural Revolution put a
stop to Muslim privileges. But today, the community is regaining its
lost ground. It has its own primary school, foodshops and restaurants
(these are popular with the Han Chinese as well). Although the
Muslims generally work on Fridays, they do observe Ramadan, the
month of fasting, from sunrise to sunset. They can often be

distinguished from the Han Chinese by their white caps and long beards.

The Great Mosque survived the Cultural Revolution virtually unscathed and remains an outstanding Chinese re-interpretation of an Islamic place of worship. It was founded in 742, according to a stone tablet in the mosque, but nothing from this Tang period survives. The present layout dates from the 14th century. Restoration work was done in 1527, 1606 and 1768. The mosque occupies a rectangle 250 metres by 47 metres (820 feet by 155 feet), divided into four courtyards. Throughout there are walls with decoratively carved brick reliefs and the buildings are roofed with beautiful turquoise tiles.

The **first courtyard**, which was restored in 1981, has an elaborate wooden arch nine metres (29.5 feet) high dating from the 17th century. Most visitors enter the mosque through a gate leading into the **second courtyard.** This contains a stone arch and two free-standing steles. One bears the calligraphy of a famous Song master, Mi Fu (1051–1107), the other that of Dong Qichang of the Ming.

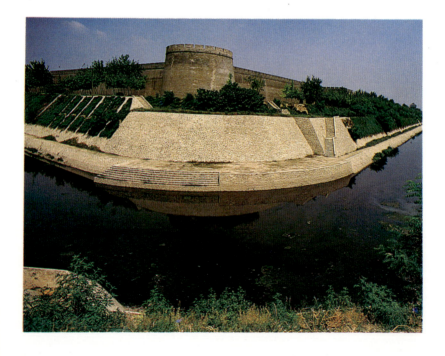

At the entrance to the **third courtyard** is a Stele Hall with tablets of the Ming and Qing periods inscribed in Chinese, Arabic and Persian. The Stele of the Months, written in Arabic by an imam in 1733, contains information about the Islamic calendar.

In the middle of the third courtyard is the minaret, an octagonal pagoda with a triple roof of turquoise tiles, known as the Shengxin Tower. On either side are sets of rooms. In one section, next to the imams' living quarters, there is a fascinating Qing-Dynasty map of the Islamic world painted by Chinese Muslims with the black cube of the Kaaba at Mecca in the centre. In the same room is kept an illuminated, handwritten Qur'an dating from the Qing Dynasty.

The **fourth courtyard**, the principal one of the complex, contains the Prayer Hall. By the entrance is a small room with an upright stele recording in Chinese the foundation of the mosque in 742. The stone itself is probably not original. In front of the entrance is the ornamental **Phoenix Pavilion** with a board proclaiming the 'One Truth' of the One God, written during the Ming. Behind the Phoenix Pavilion are two fountains flanked by two small stele pavilions and behind them is the broad, raised stone terrace used for worship.

The large **Prayer Hall** dates from the Ming; the board outside the main door was bestowed by the Yongle Emperor (reigned 1403–24). The ornate woodwork inside is mainly of this period. There is a coffered ceiling, each panel containing different Arabic inscriptions. The mihrab at the far end has some fine carving. In mid-1987 the prayer hall was undergoing extensive renovation, with most of the refurbishment being done meticulously by hand.

To walk to the Great Mosque go north along the street that passes under the Drum Tower, and take the first left. A sign in English indicates the way. It is open from 9 am to 6 pm.

The Temple of the Eight Immortals

China's indigenous religion, Daoism (Taoism), is best represented in Xi'an by the Temple of the Eight Immortals (Ba Xian An).

Located just east of the city wall, it housed 100 monks as recently as 20 years ago. But at the start of the Cultural Revolution in 1966 half the buildings were demolished, and those that remained were converted into a machine plant. Later, one of the halls was restored, and the temple is now functioning again in a small way. Several young Daoist monks work at the temple, and can be distinguished by their long hair.

Although no foundation stele exists, it is thought the temple was established during the Northern Song (960–1127). It expanded during

the Yuan and Ming, and became particularly important during the Qing. When the imperial Court was in exile in Xi'an (1900−01), the Empress Dowager Cixi grew especially fond of the temple and used to go there to paint peonies.

To get there by public transport, take trolleybus number 5 one stop beyond the wall, walk back along Changle Lu and take the first left. When that road ends, bear right and then left. The temple compound is on the right. Drivers and neighbourhood people can direct you.

Eastern Peak Temple

This Daoist complex, founded in 1116, is situated about 50 metres (55 yards) from the northwest corner of the East Gate. It is now in the grounds of a primary school and normally closed but the inquisitive visitor can sometimes persuade the caretaker to open the building for a brief look. The temple was dedicated to the cult of Tai Shan, the most important of the sacred mountains of China. Today, though all the altars have of course gone, there are still a few traces of the once-famous frescoes. A small Qing pavilion at the rear of the compound, in bad condition, has additional murals.

To walk to the temple from the East Gate, just look for the blue, lacquered roof and follow the small alleyway that leads you there.

The Temple of the Town God

Within walking distance of the Bell Tower, this temple is now a school and warehouse but some of the buildings are still in reasonable condition. A walk to the temple from Xi Dajie will take you to the interesting old Muslim quarter. The temple dates back to 1389, but was moved to its present site in 1432. It has been rebuilt and restored many times, notably in 1723 when materials were utilized from the 14th-century palace of the Prince of Qin, Zhu Shuang. The main hall, built in 1723, survives with richly carved doors and a bright blue-tiled roof.

To get there walk along Xi Dajie to number 257, then take the small lane running north through the Muslim quarter, past an active mosque on the left. Turn right at the T-intersection, then right again, down a cobbled alley. At the end of this lane turn right again into the temple gates.

Revolution Park (Geming Gongyuan)

The park, in the northeast of the walled city, is where those who died in the 1926 Siege of Xi'an are buried. Anti-Nationalist forces laid siege to Xi'an on 15 May 1926 after the city had been occupied by a pro-

Nationalist general, Yang Hucheng. Despite appalling starvation and a
fierce bombing attack, the city held out until 28 November 1926, when
the siege was finally lifted. Yang Hucheng wrote the funeral couplet
for those 50,000 inhabitants and refugees who are said to have died
during the siege:

> They led glorious lives and died a glorious death.
> Their merits are known throughout Shaanxi, as are their regrets.

The park contains a three-storeyed pagoda erected in 1927. As the
largest park within the city walls, it is very popular with the local
townspeople and especially crowded on Sundays.

The Eighth Route Army Office Museum

Near Revolution Park at 1, Qixianzhuang, just off Beixin Jie, is the
Eighth Route Army Office (initially called the Red Army Liaison
Office) which is now a museum. It was founded immediately after the
Xi'an Incident which had resulted in the Nationalists and Communists
joining forces against the Japanese (see page 102).

The office once linked the headquarters of the Communist Party in
Yan'an in northern Shaanxi with the outside world in the struggle
against the Japanese. It obtained vital supplies for Yan'an, helped
recruits make their way there, and publicized the policies of the party
leadership. The office functioned until July 1947. It is now preserved as
it was during the Sino-Japanese War.

Occupying a series of plain but attractive grey and white one-storey
buildings set around four courtyards, the museum is a good deal more
interesting than its name might suggest. There is an exhibition room
with many fascinating photographs taken in Shaanxi during the 1930s
and '40s. Visitors are also shown the rooms where important
Communist leaders, including Zhou Enlai and Deng Xiaoping, stayed.
The Canadian doctor Norman Bethune, later to become almost a cult
figure in China, was also once a visitor there.

The office still has its 1939 Chevrolet, originally imported from
Hong Kong and used for urgent missions to Yan'an. The radio room
contains the old transmitter and receiver. Even the director of the
museum is an interesting character: Tang Bin, a veteran soldier, joined
the Communist Fourth Route Army in Sichuan in 1933, when he was
only 16, and eventually became a guard at the Eighth Route Army
Office in Lanzhou from 1938 to 1946, later rising to be a company
commander in the air force. He has been the director of the museum
since 1964.

The museum is open from 9 am to 5 pm.

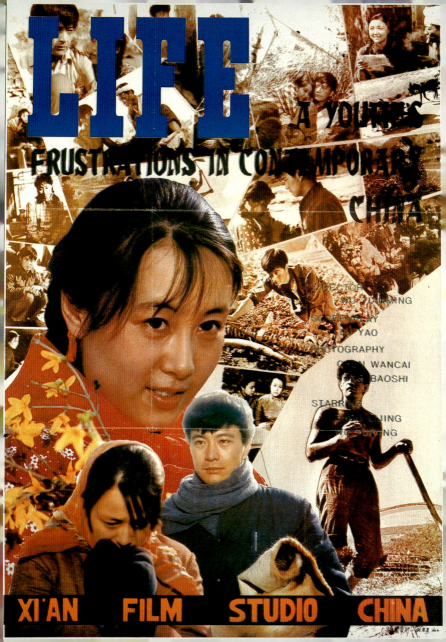

Xi'an Film Studio

In 1985 a Chinese movie, *Yellow Earth*, was hailed as the most imaginative and original film shown at the London Film Festival that year. *Yellow Earth*'s beautifully shot scenes of the loess landscape of Shaanxi, its innovative use of imagery, and the bold political stance implicit in its theme of remorselessly unchanging peasant attitudes, demonstrated a breakthrough in Chinese cinema.

The film's director, Chen Kaige, and its cinematographer, Zhang Yimou, are now working at Xi'an, although strictly speaking neither is officially employed by the film studio there. Xi'an Dianying Zhipian Chang (Xi'an Film Factory), based in a complex of unassuming buildings on Xiying Lu near the Big Goose Pagoda, is one of the newer studios that have sprung up in the provinces. It was set up in 1956 (the established studios in Beijing, Shanghai and Guangzhou were all founded before Liberation). Some 40 directors and a total staff of 1,000 produce a mix of popular films — historical romances, *kungfu* and contemporary comedies — which in turn subsidize more experimental and less commercial pictures. It is no coincidence that several of the so-called 'fifth-generation' directors (mostly young recruits to the industry from among post-Cultural Revolution graduates of the Beijing Film Academy) have flocked to Xi'an. This discernible concentration of creative energies has come about precisely because of the studio's policy of regularly sponsoring films on the criterion of their artistic potential rather than their mass appeal or propagandist content.

The exciting possibilities inherent in giving talented directors such freedom have been realized by the production of a number of controversial films which, after long deliberation by Chinese censors, have secured international release. *Life*, based on a novella by Shaanxi-born writer Lu Yao, was screened in the U.S. in 1984. *River without Buoys* by the same director, Wu Tianming (the current head of Xi'an Film Studio), was shown at the London Film Festival. Other notable examples are *Wild Mountain*, directed by Yan Xueshu, and, more recently, *The Black Cannon Incident*, directed by Huang Jianxin, which has been viewed by enthusiastic audiences in the U.S.A., West Germany and Hong Kong.

(facing page) Poster for the 1984 film Life, *which was released to coincide with the 35th anniversary of the founding of the People's Republic of China. The film explores the social gulf between town and country through the experiences of a teacher assigned to work in a backward village in northern Shaanxi.*

A Guide to Pronouncing Chinese Names

The official system of romanization used in China, which the visitor will find on maps, road signs and city shopfronts, is known as *Pinyin*. It is now almost universally adopted by the Western media.

Non-Chinese may initially encounter some difficulty in pronouncing romanized Chinese words. In fact many of the sounds correspond to the usual pronunciation of the letters in English. The exceptions are:

Initials

c is like the *ts* in 'i*ts*'
q is like the *ch* in '*ch*eese'
x has no English equivalent, and can best be described as a hissing consonant that lies somewhere between *sh* and *s*. The sound was rendered as *hs* under an earlier transcription system.
z is like the *ds* in 'fa*ds*'
zh is unaspirated, and sounds like the *j* in 'j*ug*'

Finals

a sounds like 'ah'
e is pronounced as in 'h*e*r'
i   is pronounced as in 'sk*i*'
   (written as *yi* when not preceded by an initial consonant). However, in *ci*, *chi*, *ri*, *shi*, *zi* and *zhi*, the sound represented by the *i* final is quite different and is similar to the *ir* in 's*ir*', but without much stressing of the *r* syllable.
o sounds like the *aw* in 'l*aw*'
u sounds like the *oo* in '*oo*ze'
ê is pronounced as in 'g*e*t'
ü is pronounced as the German *ü* (written as *yu* when not preceded by an initial consonant)

The last two finals are usually written simply as *e* and *u*.

Finals in Combination

When two or more finals are combined, such as in *hao*, *jiao* and *liu*, each letter retains its sound value as indicated in the list above, but note the following:

ai is like the *ie* in 't*ie*'
ei is like the *ay* in 'b*ay*'
ian is like the *ien* in 'V*ien*na'
ie similar to 'ear'
ou is like the *o* in 'c*o*de '
uai sounds like 'why '
uan is like the *uan* in 'ig*uan*a'
   (except when preceded by *j*, *q*, *x* and *y*; in these cases a *u* following any of these four consonants is in fact *ü* and *uan* is similar to *uen*.)

| ue | is like the *ue* in 'd*ue*t' |
| ui | sounds like 'way' |

Examples

A few Chinese names are shown below with English phonetic spelling beside them:

Beijing	Bay-jing
Cixi	Tsi-shi
Guilin	Gway-lin
Hangzhou	Hahng-jo
Kangxi	Kahn-shi
Qianlong	Chien-lawng
Tiantai	Tien-tie
Xi'an	Shi-ahn

An apostrophe is used to separate syllables in certain compound-character words to preclude confusion. For example, *Changan* (which can be *chang-an* or *chan-gan*) is sometimes written as *Chang'an*.

Tones

A Chinese syllable consists of not only an initial and a final or finals, but also a tone or pitch of the voice when the words are spoken. In *Pinyin* the four basic tones are marked ‾, ´, ˇ and `. These marks are almost never shown in printed form except in language texts.

Recommended Reading

History and Religion
K. Ch'en: *Buddhism in China, A Historical Survey* (Princeton University Press, Princeton, New Jersey, 1964)
J. Bertram: *First Act in China: The Story of the Sian Mutiny* (1938, reprinted by Hyperion Press, Westport, Conn., 1973)
M. Zanchen (Translated by Wang Zhao): *The Life of General Yang Hucheng* (Joint Publishing Company, Hong Kong, 1981)
E. Reischauer: *Ennin's Dairy* (Ronald Press Company, New York, 1955)
Peter Hopkirk: *Foreign Devils on the Silk Road* (Oxford University Press reprint, 1986)

Arts and Archaeology
W. Watson: *Ancient China, The Discoveries of Post-Liberation Archaeology* (BCC, London, 1974)
B. Laufer: *Chinese Pottery of the Han Dynasty* (1909, reprinted by Charles E. Tuttle, Vermont and Tokyo, 1962)

Literature
Arthur Cooper: *Li Po and Tu Fu* (Penguin Books, Harmondsworth, 1979)
Y. Inoue (Translated by J. T. Araki and E. Seidensticker): *Lou-lan and Other Stories* (Kodansha International Limited, New York and San Francisco, 1979)
E. R. Hughes: *Two Chinese Poets, Vignettes of Han Life and Thought* (Princeton University Press, Princeton, New Jersey, 1960)
Arthur Waley: *The Life and Times of Po Chu-i 772−846* (George Allen & Unwin, London, 1949)
Translated by Yang Xianyi and Gladys Yang: *Poetry and Prose of the Tang and Song* (Panda Books, Beijing, 1984)

Twentieth-Century Travellers
Violet Cressy-Marcks: *Journey into China* (Hodder and Stoughton, London, 1940)
S. Eliasson (Translated by K. John): *Dragon Wang's River* (Methuen and Company Limited, London, 1957)
R. Farrar: *On the Eaves of the World* (E. Arnold, London, 1917)
Peter Fleming: *News From Tartary* (1936, reprinted by Futura Publications, London, 1980)
F. H. Nichols: *Through Hidden Shensi* (Charles Scribner's Sons, New York, 1902)

R. Stirling Clark and A. de C. Sowerby: *Through Shen-Kan: The Account of the Clark Expedition in North China 1908−9* (T. Fisher Unwin, London, 1912)
Lynn Pan: *China's Sorrow — Journeys Around the Yellow River* (Century, London, 1985)

Useful Addresses

Airport, Xi'an City
Xiguan tel. 44529
西安飞机场　西关

Antique Store, Xi'an City
Drum Tower tel. 28797, 27187
西安市文物商店　鼓楼

Arts and Crafts Store, Xi'an City
18 Nanxin Jie tel. 28798
西安市工艺美术服务部　南新街18号

Bank of China, Shaanxi Branch
Jiefang Lu tel. 26817, 29191
中国银行陕西分行　解放路

Bei Dajie Market
Bei Dajie tel. 28305
北大街商场　北大街

**Bureau of Foreign Trade,
Shaanxi Province**
Xincheng tel. 22178
陕西省对外贸易局　新城

Chang'an Calligraphy and Painting Shop
Beiyuanmen
长安书画店　北院门

**China International Travel Service
(CITS), Xi'an Branch (administration)**
Jiefang Lu tel. 51419
中国国际旅行社西安分社　解放路

CITS (Tourist Service)
People's Mansion (Renmin Daxia)
tel. 53201
中国国际旅行社　人民大厦

China Travel Service (CTS)
Xisi Lu, tel. 21309
中国旅行社　西四路

**Civil Aviation Administration of China
(CAAC)**
296 Xishaomen (outside the West Gate),
tel. 41989
中国民航　西梢门296号

Cloisonné Factory, Xi'an City
21 Yanta Lu
西安市金属工艺厂　雁塔路21号

Dong Dajie Department Store
Dong Dajie tel. 25613
东大街百货商店　东大街

Exhibition Centre, Shaanxi Province
Longshoucun, Beijiao tel. 61781
陕西省展览馆　北郊龙首村

**Foreign Affairs Office, People's
Government of Shaanxi Province**
Visitors Reception Centre
Jianguo Lu tel. 21363
陕西省人民政府外事办公室　建国路

**Foreign Languages Bookstore, Shaanxi
Province**
Dong Dajie tel. 24414, 22197
陕西省外文书店　东大街

Foreign Languages Institute, Xi'an
Wujiafen, Nanjiao tel. 52956, 53133
西安市外语学院　南郊吴家坟

Fourth Army Hospital
Changle Lu tel. 35331, 31321, 31101
第四军队医院　长乐路

Friendship Store, Xi'an City
Nanxin Jie tel. 23749, 23898
西安市友谊商店　南新路

Friendship Taxi Company
Caochangpo tel. 717560
西安市友谊汽车公司　草场坡

Jade Carving Factory, Xi'an City
173 Xiyi Lu tel. 22085
西安市玉石雕刻厂　西一路173号

Jiaotong University, Xi'an
26 Xianning Lu (opposite Xingqing
Park)
tel. 31231, 31736
西安交通大学　咸宁路26号

Jiefang Lu Department Store
Jiefang Lu tel. 24348
解放路百货商店　解放路

Jiefang Market
Jiefang Shichang tel. 28083
解放百货商场　解放市场

Library, Shaanxi Province
Xi Dajie tel. 22420
陕西省图书馆　西大街

Long-distance Bus Stations

Yuxiang Gate Bus Station
Huancheng Xi Lu
tel. 22061
玉祥门汽车站　环城西路

Jiefang Gate Bus Station
Huochezhan Guangchang Xi tel. 24418
解放门汽车站　火车站广场西

Xiaonan Gate Bus Station
Huancheng Nan Lu, Western Section
tel. 22563
小南门汽车站　环城南路西段

**Long-distance Telecommunications
Office, Xi'an City**
Bei Dajie tel. 24007
西安长途电信局　北大街

Minsheng Department Store
Jiefang Lu tel. 26651
民生百货商店　解放路

Northwestern University
65 Daxue Dong Lu tel. 25036
西北工业大学　大学东路65号

Outer Districts Bus Station
Nanmen Wai tel. 26695
远郊汽车站　南门外

Overseas Chinese Department Store
Nanxin Jie
华侨百货商店　南新街

Post Office, Xi'an City
Bei Dajie tel. 23792
西安市邮政局　北大街

Railway Station, Xi'an City
Huochezhan Guangchang
tel. 26976, 26076
西安市火车站　火车站广场

**Special Arts and Crafts Factory,
Xi'an City**
Huancheng Xi Lu tel. 28780
西安市特种工艺美术厂　环城西路

Shaanxi Folk Art Gallery
16 Yanta Lu
陕西民间美术馆　雁塔路16号

Shaanxi Normal University
Wujiafen, Nanjiao tel. 711946
陕西师范大学　南郊吴家坟

Shaanxi Provincial Hospital
Youyi Xi Lu tel. 51331, 53261
陕西省医院　友谊西路

Index of Places

Chronology of Periods in Chinese History

Palaeolithic	c.600,000–7000 BC
Neolithic	c.7000–1600 BC
Shang	c.1600–1027 BC
Western Zhou	1027–771 BC
Eastern Zhou	770–256 BC
Spring and Autumn Annals	770–476 BC
Warring States	475–221 BC
Qin	221–207 BC
Western (Former) Han	206 BC–8 AD
Xin	9–24
Eastern (Later) Han	25–220
Three Kingdoms	220–265
Western Jin	265–316
Northern and Southern Dynasties	317–589
Sixteen Kingdoms	317–439
□Former Zhao	304–329
□Former Qin	351–383
□Later Qin	384–417
Northern Wei	386–534
Western Wei	535–556
Northern Zhou	557–581
Sui	581–618
Tang	618–907
Five Dynasties	907–960
Northern Song	960–1127
Southern Song	1127–1279
Jin (Jurchen)	1115–1234
Yuan (Mongol)	1279–1368
Ming	1368–1644
Qing (Manchu)	1644–1911
Republic	1911–1949
People's Republic	1949–